Pure F*cking Magick

Unlock Your Inner Power and Create Your New Life in 30 Days

Katie Cavenagh

Pure F*cking Magick
Copyright © 2022 Katie Cavenagh

All rights reserved. No part of this book may be used or reproduced by any means, graphic, electronic, or mechanical, including photocopying, recording, taping or by any information storage retrieval system without the written permission of the publisher, except in the case of brief quotations embodied in critical articles and reviews.

ISBN Paperback: 978-1-954493-41-4

Cover artwork: Canva
Cover design: Katie Cavenagh

This book is designed to provide information and motivation to our readers. It is sold with the understanding that the publisher is not engaged to render any type of psychological, legal, or any other kind of professional advice. The content of each article is the sole expression and opinion of its author, and not necessarily that of the publisher. No warranties or guarantees are expressed or implied by the publisher's choice to include any of the content in this volume. Neither the publisher nor the author shall be liable for any physical, psychological, emotional, financial, or commercial damages, including, but not limited to, special, incidental, consequential or other damages. Our views and rights are the same: You are responsible for your own choices, actions, and results.

Dedication

Dedicated to...

To the coffee that has kept me creative through the early mornings of writing, all the people who have, do, and will work with me that shine their light and inspire change, and to my mentors who have shown me that there's more to life than meets the eye.

I am blessed beyond belief to have been given the opportunity to share all this knowledge with the world, and I am so grateful for all the support, both in the physical and non-physical realms, that have trusted me with embodying, sharing, and teaching this information.

And lastly, this book is dedicated to all my weirdos, who have continued to listen to me talk about things that are strange and crazy, and who also dare to show up as their true unique selves. This shit ain't for the faint of heart.

Let's go change the world.

Contents

Foreword	7
Introduction	9

Part One:

Day 1: Get Clear	15
Day 2: Commit	19
Day 3: Starting Point	23
Day 4: Excavate	26
Day 5: Turn It Around	30
Day 6: Anchor It In	34
Day 7: Guided Action	38
Day 8: Talk It Up	42
Day 9: Build Trust	46
Day 10: Ask	50

Part Two:

Day 11: Contradictions	54
Day 12: Do It NOW	58
Day 13: Celebrate	61
Day 14: Clean Up Your Act	64
Day 15: Play Dress-Up	68
Day 16: Be Uncomfortable	72
Day 17: The Power Of Words	75
Day 18: Resistance	79
Day 19: Find New Friends	82
Day 20: Be A Magnet	85

Part Three:

Day 21: Create A Plan	89
Day 22: Relax	95
Day 23: Detox	99
Day 24: Remember	103
Day 25: Have Gratitude	107
Day 26: Stay Present	111
Day 27: Reflect	116
Day 28: Keep The Faith	120
Day 29: Hold Tight	124
Day 30: Be Tenacious	128

Foreword

"I need to work with you. I don't know how, I don't know why, I just have to."

    Those were the words I said to Katie after I met her in the early months of 2022. After our initial meeting, I got lost in the shuffle of work and life, like we all do. After a few months of not using my prepaid sessions with her, she reached out to see if I'd like to transfer them and do a private session (a rarity in business, that I have experienced). That communication spoke immediately to Katie's authenticity.

    Fast forward to the fall of 2022, after returning to work with Katie this past year, I am honored and blessed to introduce you to an amazing individual who through the teachings in her book, coupled with her deep wisdom and superior intellect has guided, listened, laughed, and cheered me on as I create a life I never thought I'd be living (and loving), taking risks and reaping the rewards.

    I am a self-professed life learner and by profession, a paralegal. My mindset is quite logical. I have had an amazing 18-year career and worked my way up the legal ladder. I mentor paralegals, sit on Boards and was my undergraduate class speaker at the age of 43 years old. After seemingly easy accomplishments, albeit I worked hard at everything I did both in my personal and professional lives, in 2017 a sequence of events in my life (death, divorce, family crises) occurred during the final stages of completing my undergraduate degree. I thought my life was falling apart in front of me.

    I learned through working with Katie, that all of those life events and experiences (good or bad) become the story of who you tell yourself you are. I managed to turn portions of my life around but because of my inquisitive mind and logical mindset, I wanted to find out how, why, and what to do to re-create a life that fully supported my happiness and goals. After finding Katie and her guidance, I realized it was time to "cut the crap" and figure out how to restart my "new" life with new ways.

Working with Katie empowered me to create massive transformations in my life, and shifted my perspective on how I looked at things (I worked on multiple areas.) My transformations took months, but I was dedicated to putting my life pieces back together, figuring out what I learned, seeing where I could do better, and experiencing life through different lenses.

Katie, who you will shortly find out, fills every page of her book and every moment of change you are about to embark on with crazy positive energy, constant big smiles (check out her website – she WILL actually cheer and dance with your successes), and uses the most enchanting words to express, explain, and reframe (with kindness) some of the challenges one could face. She has a magical way of walking you through a challenge, holding honesty at the forefront all while guiding you to new ways of thinking. Remember that old saying "You can't teach an old dog new tricks" — well, if that old dog wants to learn new tricks, here is the book to guide you. I am proof (logic again.)

Katie's book *Pure F*cking Magick* is a step-by-step daily guide she compiled after working through her own life. Once you embark on this journey and begin to look at your thoughts, beliefs, and patterns consciously, there is no turning back. You will wish you did this sooner. Katie's book helps you "unpack" current thoughts and

Foreword

beliefs, figure out what is no longer working for you, and challenge you WITH HOMEWORK (insert sigh here — that's the kicker) that you must do consistently to reprogram your thoughts. As you will hear Katie explain in her book, you must get rid of what's in the old space to create new space, so homework and quiet reflection time are key.

While all of this sounds amazingly easy, be prepared to do the work. You will work, work again, fall back (you must go backward in order to progress forward – a "Katie-ism"), work again, get the a-ha moment, then create space for new thoughts. You will then have to hammer and nail those new thoughts and beliefs in the new space so when familiar patterns appear (the universe will test you) your new thoughts will be your guidepost.

So, welcome to your journey! We expect to see you at the finish line and just know that Katie and your new tribe will be celebrating (and re-hammering the nails, if they fall out!) your success!

Jonna Rigon, Client & Founder/CEO of Rigon Consulting

Introduction

It's time to cut the crap.

If you've picked up this book you're probably looking for something in your life to change, and you're ready to take control of creating your reality. Manifest some miracles maybe?

We think that change has to be hard or overwhelming, and to be honest, yes, it requires some tough decisions. However, when you have a clear path to your dreams, the opportunities present themselves for you to notice and choose.

It is absolutely possible to manifest a life you love living, and it starts with the ability to be aware of what's actually going on. Getting out of the loop-cycle of thoughts rolling around in your noggin takes some conscious effort, but once you know how to do it, you'll never experience life in the same way.

This book is designed to take you through a 30-day process to open up your awareness to where you might be letting autopilot reactions, other people's beliefs and expectations, and your own fears sabotage your efforts to move forward in your life.

Habits are built in about 28 days, so staying the course will build a manifestation muscle even the Hulk would be proud of.

Wherever you're at right now is exactly where you need to be.

Are you happy with where you are?

What would need to change for you to enjoy your life to the fullest?

What is it that you want more of?

Have you been trying and trying to manifest certain things but it's just not working for you?

We're going to dig in and change all that around. You can literally transform into a new person every moment of every day, so can you imagine what would happen if you directed your attention to this for an entire month? You might become unrecognizable to even yourself!

If you've been working hard but not getting results then this is for you.

If you're wanting changes but can't seem to implement them, this is also for you.

No matter what you're looking to call into your life, these 30 days will help you anchor in a new vibration that's aligned with what you desire, and call forth all the people, opportunities, resources, support, encouragement, inspiration, motivation, confidence, and courage to make it manifest!

It doesn't matter when you start making changes in your life. You don't have to wait for a certain day or for permission.

Your life is your own journey and you get to call the shots. So many people, though, don't even know they have the ability to do this, and, if they do, they don't feel empowered to take the reins.

Each day, for 30 days, you will be given a topic, a breakdown of what it is and how to apply the information. There is an assignment for you to incorporate the wisdom and techniques into your life (and some bonus work if you're an overachiever like me).

Introduction

The first few days might be the hardest because you are going to be asked to get real honest with yourself and dive deep into parts of you that you might have been avoiding for some time. Know that it's ok to feel the resistance. We're bringing it up because awareness is the key to freedom, and once you know what's been hiding in the shadows you can work to resolve it.

The willingness to change is the first step, and by picking up this book you have alerted the Universe that things are going to be different from now on.

Change is hard only if you choose it to be that way.

Remember that you can only go one step at a time. Be present with that step, wherever you're at, and enjoy the process.

You are valuable and important, and so are your dreams and desires. You are here on a planet of manifestation to do just that — manifest — and you don't need to feel worthy or deserving of what you desire. You get to have it simply because you are here (on said planet of manifestation).

Your dreams, desires, gifts, and talents belong to you because you were meant to express them here, otherwise they'd belong to someone else.

For 30 days we're going deep within, challenging our beliefs, healing things up once and for all, and empowering ourselves to follow our hearts calling. Get crystal clear, go all in, and come out as someone brand new.

Let's dive in and get you mastering your ability to manifest anything your heart desires.

Day 1: Get Clear

So you know you want things to change... do you know what it is that you want?

Often we know what we *don't* want, however when we stay focused on the lack of lovin' it, the universe is like *OK, request heard — bring you more of what you say you don't want*. The universe is sneaky like that. It doesn't work in negatives.

This gives you the chance to know what you don't want so you can decide on what you *do* want.

You have to choose a destination in order to arrive there.

Decide 100% which direction you want to go.

When you make the decision to go all in, you put yourself into a new energy, a new frequency, or vibration, if you will. This alerts the universe to start moving things your way.

Be aware that if there's any doubt, any half-deciding on your part, you won't be able to manifest what you want.

You have to be in it to win it. Be willing to do whatever it takes, no matter what. DECIDE that you *must* do/be/have this thing. Be ready to say no to anything that stands in your way.

Get your eyes blazing like a raging bull because *you* are unstoppable.

Knowing what you want is half the battle, but knowing why you want it is the key to making it manifest easily and quickly. It's your emotional attachment to the feeling you get from having it that aligns you to the frequency that brings people, opportunities, resources, and support to make it happen.

You've got to *decide* that you will have it, and even though you don't know how you'll accomplish it, you're committed to taking the actions necessary and following inspirations from the universe. Especially when none of it makes sense.

Remember, when you change everything else around you must also change, and a little bit of focus will go a long way. Wherever you place your attention the energy grows, and the universe will start working right away for you when you're clear on what you're manifesting.

Day 1 Assignment

Today is all about making a decision. There is massive power behind a solid decision to do something, and we are going to harness that power to our advantage. Once you decide for real, the universe gets right to work. So, what is it you want to call into your life experience?

100% DECIDE on what you want and that YOU WILL HAVE IT! Walk around in that energy all day. Hold it at the forefront of your mind. Plaster post-it notes anywhere you can get them to stick. Remind yourself on a constant basis. You have *consciously chosen* to go after something that sets your soul on fire.

Day 1: Get Clear

Ask yourself what you want your life to look like? What do you want more of? How do you want to feel? Who do you want to be? What things or experiences would you like to have?

Feel into the answers you came up with for the questions above. What is it like when you think about these things? Can you see, sense, feel, know, or imagine what it's like to be this version of you?

Do you get excited or is there resistance bubbling up? Jot down what you notice (you'll be referring to this again).

Got a lot on your plate and can't seem to make a decision? Ask yourself what's the most pressing, biggest thing you want to shift? What does your gut tell you to work on? Go with that. Trust your intuition because often once you start working on one thing, other patterns will smooth themselves out and problems may get solved on their own.

Bonus Assignment:

What happens knowing that you've DECIDED? Jot down some thoughts and feelings.

You *know* there's going to be work involved, but you won't waiver. You won't give up when things get hard or when you don't know the answer. You'll do WHATEVER it takes, NO MATTER WHAT.
Yea, it's *that* important.

Write out WHY you must have/do/be this thing.

Meditate on what it feels like to be in this new space, where things already have worked out for you. See yourself as having achieved your goals and sitting pretty as an upgraded version of yourself in your new life.

What feels so good about this new version of you?

WHY will this benefit you and the people you encounter?

Imagine that every action you take powerfully connects you more and more to this new you, and feel this energy connecting with you in the moment.

Take note of how the energy of deciding makes you different.

How do you show up now that you're in this energy?

Notice what's changed throughout the day, be it the way you feel (lighter/ heavier/calm), how you walk, how you respond to people and situations, random synchronicities, or even things you can't quite put your finger on but somehow know are not the same as usual. Keep a running list for yourself.

Daily Affirmation

I consciously choose what I bring into my life.

Day 2: Commit

Now that you've sat in the energy of the decision for a day, how do you feel?

Can you make the commitment to yourself that you're going to take action for 30 days because you want change that badly? Are you ready to run face first into the flames of your fear? Is it time to finally take control and align things just the way you want them once and for all?

If so, then sign the contract.

Commit 100% that NO MATTER WHAT you will do what it takes to succeed, especially when you don't want to because you're scared, overwhelmed, or tired. These are exactly the times when you need to remember and honor your commitment to yourself to push through the tough parts. If you're not willing to do the work NO MATTER WHAT, then you haven't really decided that you 100% want what you want badly enough.

And if that stings a little, good. It's a sign that you need to get honest with yourself. Is what you're asking for *really* what you want or is it a result of someone else's expectations? Could your old self/ego be trying to talk you out of it simply because deep down you're afraid to change?

If you feel resistance to commitment, explore it.

I do this all the time, so if you feel this way know that you're not alone. I can't tell you how many times I've started something, fully making the decision to do it consciously, and then failing on my commitment to keep going.

Over the years I have come to realize there's a deeply ingrained pattern that relates to old rejection and abandonment wounds that need attention and healing. Somewhere deep in my unconscious, I don't *really* want to change because I feel like I'll be all alone (*soooo* not true in reality), so I end up holding on to those old patterns out of fear and comfort.

Check to see where you may feel the urge to talk yourself out of it and then make the commitment anyway. This is part of the decision you made yesterday. You gotta be all in.

A lot of the time we shy away from truly making the commitment because we "don't know how" things will happen or get done. We get all caught up in trying to figure out how we will make this happen, almost as if we are planning out the way we will get our end result.

The problem with this is that we *aren't supposed to know how it will happen!* This is the job of the universe, and when you decide and commit to having what you want, you must trust that things will line up for you. You are responsible for the "what" and the "why," not the "how."

With this in mind, are you willing to commit?

Day 2 assignment

Sign the contract with yourself.

Day 2: Commit

Rip it out and keep it with you. Any time you start to waiver, worry, doubt, fear, or shrink back into your old patterns, remember you made a commitment to yourself to stay the course. You *know* this is for your highest and best good. When you keep that in mind it's easier to get through those hard decisions, conversations, and tasks. You got this!

Daily Affirmation
Just for today I am willing to honor myself and my dreams.

Contract

I,

_____

am committed with my full self to the decision to

_____

I promise to myself that *no matter what* I will keep taking steps forward each day to reach my goal, especially when it's hard or uncomfortable.

I trust that I will be guided to my next steps so long as I keep myself in the energy of my decision and commitment, and consistently take action.

I create healthy boundaries around myself so I will have the support I need to succeed, and limit my exposure to those who don't share my vision or want to bring me down.

I've decided to go the distance and will do whatever it takes to make this happen for myself because it is important to me, my dreams matter, and I am a valuable member of this planet.

I play big, I play for keeps, and I play by my own rules.

I am a powerful co-creator with the Universe. I am in control of my life and energy. I am ready and willing to step up to the plate and shine like the star I am.

_____

(Sign your name)

_____

(Date)

Day 3: Starting Point

Every expert started as a beginner, and with your own personal journey it's no different. You must acknowledge and honor where you are at today, so you can celebrate your progress tomorrow. Take a moment to breathe, slow your roll, and center yourself. Where you are is exactly where you're supposed to be.

The biggest roadblock is when we get all worked up over wanting to be "somewhere else" on our journey. We tell ourselves we aren't moving fast enough, we'll never get what we want, things are too hard or overwhelming, or that we don't deserve it.

Comparison is what kills dreams.

Honoring where you are *right now* will anchor you to a starting point to compare you to you, NOT to someone else. Everyone here is on their own unique journey and trying to compare them would be like attempting to find the similarities between an elephant and an orange. Sure, they both have distinct scents, but that's about it. Just like humans — we're all in meat suits, but underneath is a multidimensional being with a very specific mission.

Our past isn't what defines us, nor does it create our future. Decisions made in the present moment create our realities, although we do have the choice to choose the same thing as we've always chosen, aka identify with our past.

As we grow and change, we can use the past as a way to measure our progress, not as a place to live and dwell. We're able to recognize old patterns when we look back and see who we were, as well as distinguish choices that we made consciously or unconsciously from a place of autopilot.

The present moment is all we have. Yesterday and tomorrow don't matter because they do not exist. Allow yourself to fully experience all that the present moment has to give you, it's all part of the journey.

Day 3 assignment

This is where we take our first measurement so we can look back on our journey over the remaining 27 days. Cozy up with a journal and get ready to be honest with yourself as you answer these questions.

What does it feel like to be in the *I'm doing this no matter what* energy of your decision?

What's different? Write down everything that you notice that's different about yourself — your energy, your thoughts, your body, the people around you, the words you say, inspiration, opportunities, etc.

It's ok if you haven't noticed anything different. How often are you asked to look for that? We're going to be using this exercise a lot as a tool to measure how we've changed, so start taking stock of what's different in your life.

How do you feel today when you think about your decision and commitment?

Amazing, excited, motivated, inspired, and ready? Great! Anchor that in.

Day 3: Starting Point

Not so much? Ask yourself:

Where are the places where fear and doubt creep in? Why?

Where am I defaulting back to an old story or limiting belief about my worth or ability to succeed? What are the stories and beliefs?

Where is there resistance to any part of my dream? Why might I be resisting?

Note whatever comes up for you — we'll be digging in later so if you'd like, keep a running list of all the things that you notice stand in your way: words, thoughts, beliefs, people, things, situations, past events, future worries.... Jot it ALL down.

And don't forget to include any of your own observations about how you feel and any other new awareness that has shown up for you, even if you don't think it makes sense.

Where you are is where you're at. When you have a solid starting point it's easy to measure your progress. Give yourself permission to be ok with wherever you're starting from. It's not a race.

When you do the work you *will* see results. Just by making and committing to a decision, you've already alerted the universe of your request, and things are starting to align behind the scenes for you. It's just a matter of time (the only unknown factor) before you start seeing proof.

Daily Affirmation
My journey is my own and I am right where I need to be.

Day 4: Excavate

Today is all about finding out what might be hiding beneath the surface.

It's time to start digging for things that make you question your beliefs, thoughts, words, feelings, and actions. Have you seriously taken stock lately of these factors and how they affect your ability to make your dreams come true?

Often we say we want something, and even take steps forward, but then it somehow comes crashing down and we give up. It's not for lack of inspiration or motivation, it's often a hidden belief in the subconscious that's really running the show, sabotaging our efforts.

Maybe we don't believe we can have it, or we say, do, or feel things that contradict what we're working towards. We tell ourselves over and over that we can't, and we reinforce that "truth" into our belief system, regardless if it's really true or not.

Subconscious beliefs from what we experienced early in childhood form the basis of how we perceive life. We can try all we want to proceed logically, using our affirmations, mantras, and positive thinking habits, however when the underlying belief driving the bus isn't addressed at the root, it will continue to play out the same cycles over and over.

Mind over matter, literally. You can't change the thought if the body is caught in a loop reaction (triggers) because they are so deeply intertwined. Remember, the

Day 4: Excavate

body holds onto everything deep within your cells. Connecting into the belief where it lives in the physical body helps to release the energy around it, creating space for you to create a new belief in its place.

This is why you experience those pesky patterns and find yourself in the same situation as always, making the same choices and wondering why nothing is changing. Your body and mind are caught in a vicious cycle when the autopilot reactions go unnoticed.

Mindset reframing is part of the solution and knowing what you're up against is half the battle. The one true way to release these beliefs is to know what they are, then go right in and *feel* them in the body. Being present with the emotion underneath will start to unravel it, freeing you from the patterns and beliefs that are holding you back.

Now that you have 100% decided you are all in, you've committed to doing the work, and have noticed physically, emotionally, mentally, and spiritually where you're starting from, it's time to start clearing the garbage.

Beliefs that you can't, won't, or don't deserve it? Garbage.

Nagging voice saying, "But I don't know how"? Garbage.

Worry about failing, succeeding, being seen, or heard? Garbage.

Using the past as an excuse to not move forward? Garbage.

Scared about pissing people off who don't support you anyway? Garbage.

You get the point.

Remember, awareness is the key to freedom and you can't solve a problem if you don't know it's there. When you are shining the light of your consciousness on something, you can observe it from multiple angles, and sometimes watch it dissolve from just being present with the energy.

Day 4 assignment:

This step requires you to dig a little deeper under the surface and be honest with yourself about where you're at. As you answer the following questions, trust yourself and the process to reveal things that need to be acknowledged, recognized, and healed.

Yesterday you noticed what came up for you as far as resistance. Do you notice any patterns? We're going to unpack some of that resistance, so keep noticing what happens in your body when you ask yourself these questions (you might also want to journal your thoughts).

- Why do you want what you want?
- How will it change your life when you achieve it?
- Why do you think you haven't brought it into your life yet?
- What have you been saying about it? (List all positive and negative phrases that fly out of your mouth or across your mind)
- What do you believe about it and your ability to do/be/have it?
- Are these beliefs true? Are they even yours? Where did they come from?

- What would you rather believe?
- What are your excuses for not moving forward or making changes?

Taking some time to get really honest with yourself helps uncover the truth beneath the surface. The beliefs we carry around often aren't even ours, so distinguishing between them helps with the creation of a new, more empowered belief system.

Journal any other thoughts about this exercise and how your beliefs have or have not been serving you thus far.

Daily Affirmation
Beliefs are just thoughts I continue to think, and thoughts can be changed

Day 5: Turn It Around

A little awareness goes a long way. Once you've acknowledged and shed light on your saboteurs, you have brought them into your consciousness and will be able to sense when they rear their ugly heads.

What do you notice about who you've been now that you've unearthed some of your BS? Can you see how these excuses, lies, limiting beliefs, programs, and conditioning have been holding you back? Are you able to recognize how these patterns show up and sabotage your success?

Now that you know what you're dealing with, you can deal with it.

All too often we get wrapped up in our heads, believing the useless nonsense rolling around inside.

We've been conditioned to believe that we need to remain one way our whole lives, and our ego's relentless efforts to keep us "safe" within our comfort zone paralyzes us with fear when we think about taking those big, scary steps towards our dreams.

We tell ourselves over and over that we are who we are, and reinforce the beliefs we have about ourselves with our stories that we rarely change. Continuing to talk about yourself in a way that perpetuates your own loop-cycle is often tough to catch, but this is where the awareness comes in handy.

Offering ourselves a perspective shift is a sure fire way to change what we experience in our reality. If we keep going the way we're going without noticing any turn signs in the road, it's a sign that we're unconsciously choosing the same things again and again. Noticing the things we say, think, feel, and do gives us the opportunity to choose something different — even if we don't do it — and that's what starts the healing process.

Sometimes, other people get in the way because they don't want you to change. If *you* change, it changes *their* reality. A lot of people aren't willing to handle that big of a shake up and try to keep you as who you were so their world can remain comfortable.

Watch out for these sneaky patterns, programs, and conditioning, and be aware of how you respond. You may notice a tightness in your chest when you are around certain people or a knot in your stomach when charging for your services. Maybe your heart flutters at the thought of having hard conversations or asking for what you want.

Any time you feel angst, stress, tension, tightness, or anything other than love or neutrality, it's a sign healing is needed. Your awareness alone may be all it needs to find its way out. However, sometimes you may need to give yourself a hand and reset your vibration.

Words have massive power so give attention to what you say. Are you hooking into your old excuses and thought patterns and believing the lies? Do you reinforce your saboteurs by saying things like, *"Yup, that's me, the broke girl who has to shop at the Dollar Store,"* or *"Ugh, I look like I went dumpster diving this morning, jeez!"*

If you're stacking up contradictions like moving boxes, you're going to want to stop that.

Day 5 assignment:

What's your biggest excuse or belief that's in your way?

Break it down and rewrite it so that it's more useful to you. Remember, what we tell ourselves is what creates our reality, so if you're constantly saying things like, "*I could never afford that*" or "*I'll never find love,*" that's what you're speaking into existence for yourself — never having money or love.

Turning it around is much more useful as you will be speaking *towards* what you want rather than against it. Words are extremely powerful, so choose words that fit best for you.

For example,

Excuse: *I feel weird charging money for my services.*

Rewrite: My gifts and talents are meant to be shared with the world. I am on a planet that requires money to live here. I charge what I'm worth and trust the right people will find me. I am grateful for the abundance of wealth from doing my work in the world.

The key to the rewrite is to put it in words that make your bones buzz. It's got to resonate on that deep a level, otherwise you won't really believe it.

It's your beliefs that run the show, so when you notice those old thoughts creeping in, you can stop them at the gate and slip in your newly rewritten mantra to take its place.

Then, because you're changing your words, thoughts, and beliefs, you will start to notice you feel differently, and things around you will start to shift. What can you reframe into a more positive, more powerful thought? Write it out and keep it with you all day so you can refer back to it. Just choose one or two to work with at a time, you'll be circling back to this again!

Reflect:

Notice what happens when you put your focus on this new mantra. How do you show up differently? How do you feel physically and emotionally?

What new inspiration or awareness is available to you today because you've created space for it to come in? You might want to keep a running list of all the inspired thoughts or synchronicities that show up over the next few weeks.

Daily Affirmation
I consciously create my future

Day 6: Anchor It In

Have you anchored in the feeling of being a new, upgraded version of yourself? The one where you've achieved your dreams and goals, and are living life just the way you want?

The key to manifestation besides getting clear and taking action, is to *feel* into the essence of your desire. We're told to "let go" of the outcome so that we can create space for it to come to us, but a huge part of letting go that's left out is *feeling* that it's already done.

Once you can tap into the feeling of how your life will be, then you powerfully draw that frequency to you because your mind doesn't know what's real and what's imagined. We create our reality based on how we feel, so when we are in alignment and feeling positive about having something, it comes in more easily than if we felt "bad" about getting it.

If you're feeling doubt, fear, worry, or any angst about making your dreams a reality, then you are stopping the energies from reaching you. Feeling a little fear around something is normal, but if it sends you running down the street when you think about your future life, you might want to spend some time healing whatever that's all about.

Creating space for what you want is paramount if you think you're going to get it. You need to clear the room for the big sofa just like you need to clear your energy from the gunk you're holding on to.

Day 6: Anchor It In

As you clear out the old, you can anchor in the new by visualizing and feeling into your new life. When you use this practice you physiologically change your body. You are giving your cells new instructions and reprogramming your subconscious to work for you in a whole new way.

By allowing yourself to fully be in "the future you," your mind will start looking for proof of this new reality that's being created in the moment — remember your choices today make up what you experience tomorrow. Because you've anchored a new frequency into your body, your subconscious beliefs have shifted, and your reality has changed.

There's a ton of science on this and if you'd like to dig deeper I'd suggest looking into the works of Dr. Bruce Lipton, Dr. David R. Hawkins, and Dr. Joe Dispenza.

For now, suffice it to say that when you put yourself "into the future" (all possibilities exist now, but humans experience time in a linear way), you are pulling that timeline possibility to you, and as you notice your feelings of this new version of you in your day to day life, things from this new timeline can start showing up. Because you are observing the feeling of it already being done, that's the vibration you're sending out, and therefore that's what *has* to be delivered back to you.

We're living in a quantum reality where we observe things into our reality. You've got to believe it to see it. So what do you believe, and more importantly, how do you *feel* about what you are calling in?

Day 6 assignment:

How does it feel now that you've started making some changes to your mindset around your ability to take control of creating your life? Notice what's different about the way you've been showing up this week.

How do you expect to feel when you've accomplished what you've set out to do in these 30 days? Even if you don't immediately receive what you've asked for (you *do* have to be realistic with your requests knowing time is the X factor), how does it feel to have opened the gates to make the changes necessary to allow it in?

How do you expect to feel when everything is said and done?

Tap into that feeling of it all being done already. Allow yourself to fully be immersed in that feeling. Let your body soak it all up and in. Feel it in your cells and how it makes you come alive. Feel the sense of accomplishment, empowerment, and joy. Sit in that for as long as you can.

Repeat your dreams and desires to yourself and others that support you as often as you can. Keep the energy up around being that version of yourself that's already achieved your dreams.

Bonus Exercises:

1. Try on a New Suit

Can you imagine walking through your day as this person? How would they think? Speak? Act? Do they walk

Day 6: Anchor It In

or dress differently? Could you do something today that this version of you would do? Have a day of dress-up and pretend.

You might be amazed at the results, even if you just put on hard pants (like what you'd wear to the office) before checking emails for the day, because that's what the "new you" would be doing.

2. A Perfect Day

Use a visualization meditation to help you step into this future energy. Create a "day in the life" journal entry of how you would show up for a perfect day in your new life. Get really detailed and make it exactly as you want it, no judgments allowed! Step inside as you're writing or visualizing and *feel* your day happening. Let yourself walk through it, fully present, as if it's already done.

Anchor in the feeling of why you want what you want and how it will improve your life. This is holding on to the *essence* of your desire and is what raises your frequency to match your dreams.

Daily Affirmation
When I believe I can have what I want, proof shows up for me.

Day 7: Guided Action

Yesterday you stepped into the energy of "it's already done" and today we're using that energy to connect with the Divine/Source/Higher Intelligence/God/the Force — whatever you want to call the connection to that underlying invisible thread of life that's way smarter than us.

When you're connected and holding steadfast to your "why," the universe conspires to make help available to you so you can take the necessary steps to achieve your dreams. This appears in your life as synchronicities and what we might call "coincidences."

Quite often, though, we miss this divine guidance because we aren't listening, think we know better, or are just downright afraid to go there. Trusting your intuition isn't always easy if you're not used to it.

The universe whispers to us all the time with suggestions and inspiration on what we can do to be that highest version of ourselves, and will plant lessons, people, challenges, and tests in our path to make sure we're serious and on track.

This divine guidance is meant for our highest good, even if it doesn't seem like it at the time.

When you're connected to Source and your "why," you are emitting a powerful frequency that says "bring this to me now", which allows help to show up for you. Take note of all possible help that shows up for you —

Day 7: Guided Action

people, resources, opportunities, support, feelings, inspiration, etc.

As help arrives, are you willing to accept it? So many times the universe presents you with all the ingredients you need, yet you can't seem to whip together the recipe because you are expecting it to come already finished.

Can you recognize that guidance and assistance are available and beckoning you to follow along? Are you open to changing things up a bit and taking risks in order to get what you want in life? Do you see the steps appearing as you start following the path with blind faith?

Climbing the staircase to your destiny may seem long, arduous, and overwhelming. There's a Chinese proverb that reminds us "the journey of a thousand miles begins with the first step," and you can only go one step at a time. Wherever you are, be fully there and present in the moment. You're being asked to enjoy the process of progress.

Where can you find the message in the mess or step up and take a new action to move you forward? Remember, not every inspiration is a physical action to take, sometimes it's about energetically clearing something to make space to receive your next packet of information.

Day 7 assignment

Go back and reconnect with your "why." Write it out so you can anchor it in even deeper. Repetition is a key component of strengthening your connection, and each time you write out your dreams, feel into them with your whole body. Get this into your cells so you are literally operating at the deepest level possible.

Ask, *Why do I desire to do/be/have [fill in the blank]? What will it do for me to achieve this?*

Stay present today. Take note of any information you receive. It can show up in a plethora of ways such as:

- Inspirational pings (notice where you are and what you're doing when you get these)
- People showing up with some information for you
- A new opportunity
- New awareness or perspective shift
- A feeling that you should do something/take action
- A song
- A page in a book
- Something you hear on the TV or radio
- Animals or nature
- Something you uncover from journaling or meditation
- And flicker of light or awareness

When you notice these little 'love notes' from the universe, are you willing to follow them? They're showing up for you so that you will be led to take action, and will keep showing up for you in different ways until you do.

Your task today is to follow that inspiration and guidance *wherever* it may lead you. No excuses.

You can't screw up what's meant for you, and it will find its way to you regardless, so just for today allow yourself to open up to what the universe is saying and play along. What's the worst that could happen? You actually succeed in doing something new? You grow a little bit? You surprise yourself and others?

If people can turn selling ugly holiday sweaters and goat yoga into a thing because they followed the divine guidance they received with absolute trust and blind faith, you can make *your* dreams a reality too.

Step up and step in. Today you're becoming more of who you were always meant to be.

Daily Affirmation
Just for today I will notice and follow the guidance I am given by the universe.

Day 8: Talk It Up

Words are very powerful — you are literally casting a spell every time you speak. The way you word your requests to the universe can make or break you, so today we're taking a look at how your words are influencing your results and ability to succeed in the first place.

Did you know your body is about 70% water and that when you speak to yourself you are giving your body directions on what to do?! (Check out Dr Emoto's water crystal and rice experiments).

What you say has a direct effect on the way your cells function, their health, and their ability to help you move forward and level up. Your words can work for you (constructive energy) or against you (destructive energy). What you say is what you get, and when you align the energy of your words towards what you desire, you open yourself up to receive. Your words create your reality, and the way you tell yourself to show up, whether you do it consciously or unconsciously, creates your experience. So, are you talking yourself up in a way that drives your cells to fall in line and kick some ass, or are you shutting yourself down, preventing your awesomesauce from shining through?

Let's find out.

Think about your goal from day one. Now, immediately notice what your next thoughts are.

Day 8: Talk It Up

Are you talking yourself out of it right away? Saying that you can't do it or don't know how? Are you resisting or making excuses? Do you have the confidence and courage to go on or are you thinking about quitting and hiding under a box?

If these thoughts pop up, that means you're totally normal and can use a quick mindset reframe.

We have to be our biggest cheerleaders and that starts with our ability to personally motivate ourselves to do the things we need to do in order to get the things we want in life.

We can say we want something until we're blue in the face, but if our words are out of alignment with the energy of our beliefs, we're not going to get too far along at the manifestation station.

We can start to change those pesky destructive beliefs by opening up a crack with the power of our words. Our beliefs are sometimes like a brick wall where nothing can get through no matter how "hard" you work to tell yourself "yes you can." If you don't truly believe it, there's no chance of it happening.

However, when you insert a softener, you start a crack in the brick wall that will allow a new vine to infiltrate the system and take root (you've seen the flowers that grow in cracks, this is the same idea). Using words like "willing," "open," or "even though" allows you to give yourself a chance to believe something new, rather than just shutting down the ability to try before you start.

Day 8 assignment:

Write out your reasons for wanting to change. (Remember, repetition helps anchor in your connection to the essence.)

Find at least three words that resonate with you on a deep soul level, that sum up your reasons.

For example: *I am changing my money mindset because I am sick and tired of being a slave to money and always feeling like there's never enough. I can welcome in big huge paychecks so I can have the financial freedom I desire, and be able to bless others because of my good fortune. I can be more me with money as well as be more creative in the ways I can serve the planet and humanity. It is aligned that I share my gifts and talents and charge money for my services.*

Resonating words: Freedom, feel good, share

Let's supercharge those words and create mantras that help speak to what you're creating, opening up your belief that you absolutely can have what you want.

If there are any limiting beliefs that are sabotaging your success, this is how to start turning them around so they serve you better.

Rewrites:

"Even if I don't know how, I am creating my path to financial freedom"

"Every day I am healing my relationship with money, and am willing to feel good about loving money openly and fully."

"I am willing to share my gifts and talents now, knowing the good I put out in the world will come back to me."

Now you can use these mantras if you start to feel like you're coming apart from your commitment. Things

Day 8: Talk It Up

can go awry, and if that happens, just hop back on the wagon where you fell off. NBD.

When you can't quite get fully on board, sometimes you need a stepping stool. Rewriting anything that doesn't deeply resonate is the way to open the door to changing a stubborn belief that keeps you stuck.

Daily Affirmation
I am willing to believe something different is possible for me, even if I don't know what it is.

Day 9: Build Trust

Do you have unshakable faith in your ability to pull off your dreams? Do you 100% believe that you absolutely can and will make things happen for yourself? Do you trust in your ability to follow the guidance you receive? Do you trust in your dreams becoming a reality in the first place?

Sometimes we mistakenly think our dreams are impossible and lose faith they will happen at all, especially if they're BIG dreams, like creating massive change in the world, or having a crazy idea like the Wright Brothers and flying.

And I say, if you're going to dream, you might as well go big. We only *think* things are impossible, but it's only our craptastic belief that it's not possible that stops us.

Often we lose our faith and trust in the universe because we are in a hurry for results. We "do the work" and nothing happens (or so we think). We become frustrated because we are trying to control the outcome to happen the way we want it to (when in reality it never goes the way we think it will).

This is actually resistance! Digging up the seeds you just planted is a telltale sign that you're not trusting the process. We have no control over the timing, although we *can* control what we do while we wait.

Trust is where it's at. It's how the magick happens.

Day 9: Build Trust

When you trust, you are in an open state of flow of giving and receiving. You are saying yes to divine timing and inspiration. You embrace the process and are not attached to the outcome because you *know* it's coming. So long as you do the work, look for proof, and feel the gratitude of it already being here, you are aligning with the frequency of your desire.

Gratitude is the fast track to trust.

You're trusting it'll show up by excitedly looking for proof it's already here. By doing your work with love in your heart, you are trusting the process, unattached to the outcome, ultimately creating space for what you want. Giving thanks for each step of the way is a chance to strengthen your connection, raise your frequency, and lock in with your dreams and desires. Being thankful for receiving your request, even before it's been fulfilled, shows the universe that you absolutely believe you can have what you desire. It shows that you not only trust your request was heard, but that it's also on the way to your awaiting open arms right now

Part of building trust is showing up again and again for yourself and your dreams. Following divine guidance and inspiration with blind faith every single time. Stepping out of your comfort zone often and doing things regardless if you're scared. Looking for the synchronicities and signs (or perhaps even asking for signier signs too). Things like that.

Consistently taking these actions will strengthen that trust muscle so you can be in the flow and receive the assistance you asked for.

Day 9 assignment

What's your trust level?

Take a look back over your week. What actions have you taken that were based on faith? Have you done anything that pushed your limits? Jot down some notes on where you've trusted your intuition and followed the guidance the universe presented you with.

Now, let's dig a little deeper.

Trust is something that's built, and like a muscle, the more you work it the stronger it gets. It's not always easy to put all your faith into something unknown, but when you truly believe you can do/be/have it, that trust supercharges you to be a receiving machine. This level of faith clears space immediately for you to welcome in your dreams.

Ask yourself the following questions and explore your answers and how they make you feel.

- On a scale of 1-10, how much do I trust the Universe will bring me what I asked for? Why?
- How much do I trust in my ability to work with the Universe to make my dreams a reality?
- Where have I broken trust with myself, and how can I repair it?
- Why do I trust in/not trust the Universe?
- Am I willing to put all my faith in my dreams and myself, even if I have zero proof I will succeed and/or it will work? Why?
- Where am I not trusting the process?

Day 9: Build Trust

- Has my faith wavered? Where and why?
- What can I do to strengthen my ability to trust myself and the Universe?
- What patterns from the past might still be at work sabotaging my ability to trust?

Remember, every step counts. Trust the process and where you're at. Build and strengthen that faith wherever and however you can. Know deep down that you absolutely can and will make your dreams come true, so long as you have faith that you can do it. Progress is progress.

Daily Affirmation
I trust myself and the universe.

Day 10: Ask

If you never ask, the answer will always be no.

Today is all about opening up a little more to receive all the good that is coming your way.

Have you made a formal request to the Universe alerting it of your big dreams and desires? Is it worded in a way that's supercharged —meaning the words resonate deeply and it's geared towards creating something?

The Universe requires specifics, so double check that your request is asking for what you *really* want. Keep in mind the universe doesn't understand negatives and you need to word your requests appropriately.

Then keep asking!

You never know what will show up, so just ask for anything and everything you want. If you *don't* ask, you will always receive nothing, and since this is planet manifestation, you might as well ask for what you want.

There are many ways to ask and place requests. You can do this in the physical plane and ask people for things like help, support, opportunities or jobs, money, resources, etc.

And you can ask the Universe to help you out by bringing you everything else, and dropping miracles in your lap. Anything that's out of your control you can just leave to the cosmos and ask it be taken care of while you physically do what you can take action on.

Asking requires open-ended questions, and my favorite way to ask is "What would it take for *[fill in the*

Day 10: Ask

blank] to show up?" Another good one is "What vibration do I need to be on to have *[blank]*?"

Specifics help, but if you're overly specific you run the risk of not actually getting what you want because you're cutting off the energy of all possibilities and may be pushing away something even better than you could ever imagine.

This is the main reason to just keep asking. The essence of your desire still shines through, but the things you're asking for change, as does the *way* you ask. Sometimes it's just about finding the right question, so if you're not seeing things show up for you, change the question and see what happens.

Day 10 assignment

Start asking for *everything* if you're not already. Whenever you think of it, ask for it. Ask for it multiple ways. Ask the same question 30, 40, 50 times if it's a good one that really resonates. Ask all day, every day.

For example if you're looking to bring in more money you can use the following examples. Don't simply ask for "more money" because the universe might drop a nickel in your path and tick the box as "request fulfilled".

What would it take to generate $250 today?
What would it take to manifest $1000 today?
What would it take to have multiple steady streams of income?
What would it take for one person to buy my product/service today?

What would it take to find $10?
What would it take for my next $1500 to show up?
What if I were super rich?
What would it take to have all the money I need and more?
What if money came to me easily and effortlessly?
What would it take to have my dream job?
What if my bank account was overflowing with cash?
What would it take to receive $20 or better today?
What would it take to have so much money I had to give a lot of it away because I don't need it?
What would it take to have a money miracle this week?
What if I were a master receiver of money?
What would it take for me to improve my relationship with money?
Who would I be if I LOVED money?
What financial assistance is available to me today?
What can I learn about money today?
What would it take to find the right person to teach me about investing?

And this is just the tip of the iceberg! You can have a lot of fun with this. There is nothing too big or too small, so ask for it all!

If this seems overwhelming, don't fret. Once you get a few questions down, you open the gates for your creativity to flow. Just allow whatever needs to come through to come through. Have fun brainstorming. Usually one question will lead to another, and another, and another.

Day 10: Ask

Bonus:

What questions are you currently asking the Universe? Are they communicated in a way that's conducive to receiving help?

What other requests can you make surrounding your goal for these 30 days? Write them ALL down and keep them close by. Any time you think of your goal, ask some questions around it and see what shows up.

Is there also a way you can put these requests into motion by taking a physical action? What other questions and requests can you think of that fellow humans could help you with?

You HAVE to ask for what you want in order for it to show up, then open yourself up to receive. Part of receiving is clearing energetic space for what you want to come in, another part is being the catalyst and taking guided action for your request to be fulfilled. That guidance comes from listening to the answers whispered from the universe when they show up as inspiration.

Daily Affirmation
No request is too big or too small. I am willing to boldly ask for what I want.

Day 11: Contradiction

When you say you want something, have 100% decided, are taking guided action, focusing your energy on it already being done, and keeping yourself open to receive, you are aligned with having said thing. However, if you speak, think, or act against it, you won't get the results you're looking for. The universe is *always* listening and delivering.

Take a look also at where you might be contradicting yourself by using the words "but," "if," "when," "then" as you are speaking about what you want. (*"I am making money, **but** it's really slow and tough in these times," "I can't wait to make more money, because **then** I'll be happy."*)

Also take a look at your actions. If you say you want something, how are you physically showing up for it? Are you acting in a way that opens you up to receive by saying yes to the new opportunities and guided inspiration, or are you shutting yourself down, hiding from the gifts the Universe has for you?

Are you saying no to new things or turning down opportunities to be a new person? How would the future version of you act? Are you doing any of those things now? What are ways you could incorporate some of those actions into your life today?

How do you *feel* about what it is you're asking for? If you can't really feel into the fullness of the experience of having what you want, you might have some limiting beliefs about your ability to create or receive it.

Day 11: Contradiction

If it feels scary, that's totally normal. Anything new or big and exciting is a bit scary. But if there's shame, guilt, worry, doubt, anger, resentment, or anything that feels icky or resistant, you're going to need to acknowledge that before you can truly align with the vibration you need to be on to be a new version of yourself.

You also need to check your beliefs because something hidden under the surface may be sabotaging you.

If you feel any resistance, fear, doubt, worry about achieving your goals (and it's all normal), then it's time to dig deep and clear out the fog that's blocking your path forward.

The way you feel is actually what lets you know what frequency you're on, so if you're not feeling good about what you want, there's very little chance of it actually being able to come to you. You wouldn't be able to bring money to you if you feel all weird about having it, right?

So think about it for a minute — what *do* you feel about your goals, your ability to turn them into a reality, and how things have been going so far? Do you need to upgrade your thoughts so you feel better?

What you think about is what you bring about so it's important to get your thoughts aligned with what you want. Contradicting thoughts, beliefs, words, feelings, and actions are a sure fire way to keep things out of your reach.

Day 11 assignment

Take a close look at what you're saying, thinking, feeling, and doing. This will lead you directly to your belief about something. Your beliefs run the show, so any contradicting beliefs you have about your success will then lead you right to your lessons.

There's always a message in the mess, so what are you willing to dig to uncover?

Spend some time today noticing yourself and how you respond to life. Are you living *for* what you want or for what you *don't* want? Notice where you are leaning towards what you want (saying yes, trying new things, putting yourself out there) and where you're resisting (saying no, denying yourself, avoiding, lying about false benefits, etc.).

Make a list of all the places you're speaking against yourself. How can you change your words around to reflect a more positive circumstance? How often are you saying *if, then, when, but* with your request? How are you speaking about yourself to others? Are you talking down your dreams or your ability to make them a reality? Reframe what you need to.

Notice your thoughts. What are the dominant thoughts around you having what you want? Is there a nagging voice in the background that says "no, you can't"? Are there thoughts of being unworthy or undeserving about your success? Write down what goes through your mind and determine if these thoughts are useful or not. Write out new mantras for yourself to refocus your attention.

Day 11: Contradiction

Pay attention to your feelings. Anywhere you feel angst or tightness when you think about your dreams and desires is a sign there's something to heal. Allow yourself to fully be with any fears or emotions that come up for you. They just want to be acknowledged so the energy can start moving. The awareness starts the healing process.

Anywhere you find yourself at odds with what you want is a spot you can explore. Get curious about why you feel this way and make the necessary adjustments to move forward. There's nothing "wrong" with contradicting yourself, we all do it, but when you can catch yourself and make a new choice, you are allowing yourself to expand and step more into alignment.

Daily Affirmation
I align my words, thoughts, beliefs, feelings, and actions with what I want.

Day 12: Do It NOW

What's really stopping you from diving in and living your life?

It's time to stop letting the illusion of fear keep you playing small. You've decided to go for it, and now it's time to walk the walk. It's time for a big leap forward.

The day you made your decision, the Universe started to move things around in your favor. You've probably been feeling more inspired and motivated to do the things you know you need to do.

By now you may know some more of your steps, or have already taken some big steps forward. Perhaps you've only been dipping your toes in the smaller action steps because there's still a lot of fear. Wherever you are is where you're at, and you're being asked to just honor and accept this moment for what it is. There's no judgment. There's no comparison. It's not a competition.

You probably also know that you still have to take action to set the energies in motion, creating those ripples that call forth the vibrational match. Waiting until you feel "a little more ready" is just delaying your dreams. Screwing things up isn't possible when it's meant for you, and it will find its way regardless.

You've followed your gut and have gotten to here. Have you received any inspiration or thoughts about what's possible for you? Have you had ideas about steps you could take? Big, scary, exciting things you'd love to do because you can *feel* how good it would be to do them?

Day 12: Do It NOW

Starting a podcast, leaving your soul sucking job or relationship, bonding with family, selling your awesomesauce to the world? Maybe traveling, apologizing and making amends, writing a book, or stand up comedy? Anything that lights you up and makes you get the warm fuzzies or that you absolutely *know* deep down you need to do to feel better?

Take the opportunity and do it if it's a one-stepper, or take the first step of the thousand mile journey if it's a long hauler. Don't wait. Do it NOW.

The reason for taking action when you get the inspiration, and taking the big scary steps, is because this is how you grow. You're alerting the Universe that you're ready to be rewarded for your risk. It might not always work out how you expect or want (it rarely does), but seeing everything for the value of the experience is what it's all about.

Stop dilly dallying. Stop denying yourself the opportunity to grow. If you want your dream life you have to be willing to work for it. You'll be assisted by the Universe, but *you're* the one that has to take the action.

Day 12 assignment:

What's something you know you need to do? Do iiiiiiitttttt!

Face your fear and take a step towards what you want. What are you waiting for? Stop delaying. Count yourself down 5,4,3,2,1 and just GO! Check out *The 5*

Second Rule by Mel Robbins for more on using this super helpful technique.

Stop waiting for things to get better or to feel ready. Take a baby step if you have to. Do the thing you really, *really* don't want to do.

Do. The. Thing.

Instead of thinking about failing or what you could lose, start thinking about all you will gain and how your life (and you) can blossom. Make a list if you have to.

Allow the fear to be there. Hold its hand. Be there fully with it. But do the thing anyway with blind faith that you will be supported by the universe. Trust that what you need will show up for you.

How badly do you want your dream life?

Go do the thing.

Now.

Why are you still here?

Daily Affirmation
I burn my fear with the flame of my passion and do what needs to be done, even if I am scared.

Day 13: Celebrate

Take a deep breath. You did a thing! (You *did* do it, right? Or did you talk yourself out of it with your lame excuses again? If you didn't do it, you gotta go do it now or moving on today isn't going to help you.)

Ah, there we go, take another deep breath and give yourself a pat on the back for stepping outside of your comfort zone. How does it feel to have taken a big, scary step forward? Did you wait until the last minute or did you push through your fear and do it right away?

In all honesty, I waited and let my excuses get the best of me. Yes, I am human too, and even I still deal with my old ways, which is why I created this book.

But I got up today and did the thing because I know how important this is to me. If I don't take massive action sometimes, I know I won't be where I want to be at all, so I might as well just do it.

Fear is only an illusion, yet we let it get the best of us in so many situations. Instead of getting your panties in a wad and freaking out about how something will get done or work out, just call the fear out for what it is, acknowledge you're scared, and just do the thing anyway. You usually find out it wasn't that bad in the first place, and now that you've done it, you can step into that new sense of empowerment and give yourself a big woot woot!

Inspiration comes to us all day long, and when we listen and take action, we get a swift boost from the Universe in the sense of a "rush" or a "high" of a good feeling. *That's* the special sauce of manifestation and right where you want to be.

Passing on the inspiration equates to you abandoning yourself and reinforces the lack of trust you're trying to kick to the curb. It's all about keeping that faith strong and listening to what the Universe is telling you to do. Literally the next steps are laid out in front of you when you start doing something, *anything*, that moves you towards your dreams with the blind faith that because you are being guided to do it, there is something in it for you.

What did you learn about yourself when it came to taking a giant step forward and putting yourself out there?

Day 13 assignment:

Go back and take stock of everything you've done the past almost two weeks. Make a list of all the action steps you took. List all the new awareness you have received about yourself. Jot down any synchronicities or coincidences you've experienced.

Reread Day 3 and see what's different now. Celebrate how far you've come because you are definitely *not* the same person you were when you started.

Celebrate the steps you've taken, both big and small. Celebrate *all* the things.

When you are your own cheerleader you empower yourself to keep going. You are not motivated by external validation, though you will receive it, it's not what you

Day 13: Celebrate

rely upon to determine your success. Success is an inside job, as is happiness, and they come from your perception of YOU.

Today you are celebrating YOU (NO EXCUSES!). Celebrate your unique approach to life, your unique gifts and talents, and everything you've done to step more fully into that uniqueness.

Make a list of all your great accomplishments. You can go back two weeks or two years, the timeframe doesn't matter. Write out why it's so awesome to be you. Do something nice for yourself.

There is only ONE you on the entire planet. If *that's* not something to celebrate, I don't know what is.

Daily Affirmation
I honor and celebrate the unique, creative being I am.

Day 14: Clean Up Your Act

The act of physically cleaning up your space can do wonders for you. From new inspiration to clarity (literally and figuratively), your environment sets you up for success more than you know.

If your space is cluttered, it's likely your mind is cluttered too, and perhaps you're overwhelmed and can't make a decision about something. Having a clean space to work, live, and create in will also help motivate you when you are feeling stuck or when you're on the brink of leveling up.

Now, some organized chaos can often be creative genius at its finest, but clutter that causes you anxiety or takes your focus and time away from your dreams is a beast of a different color.

Is that pile of papers turning what used to be your dining room table (which hasn't been seen in months) into the town's next ski resort? How about the laundry that's been waiting patiently to be folded for over a week, maybe two? The *junk drawer*. Is that anxiety I smell?

Realistically, how long would it take to clean up a small corner, fold and put away a basket of clothes, or even just toss some old papers and junk mail? Alternatively, you could set a timer for an hour and see what you can get through. I'll bet you'll be pleasantly surprised at how amazing you'll feel afterwards.

What about painting the bedroom to switch things up? Buying new towels for the bathroom? When was the

Day 14: Clean Up Your Act

last time you used the good new luxurious sheets usually reserved for guests, or cleaned your closet or car?

The simple act of changing something around, cleaning, going all out redesign, or even just fluffing the pillows gets stagnant energy moving.

Setting up your space to reflect your dreams is also a way to motivate you to keep going.

Seeing something that inspires you everyday reminds you of why you're committed to making it happen. This helps raise your vibration, and by allowing yourself to feel those good feelings that come to you when you think of having what you want, you open the space for more.

Reflecting your future self and situation in your current environment helps you step up and into the next level version of you. If you're wanting to be a high level, high-powered CEO, but you're only at entry level, perhaps you start with a nice desk chair, nameplate, business cards, or office.

Clear out the clutter of anything that doesn't point you forward, and set yourself up for success. How would the new you live? What would they have? How do they relax and unwind?

It's incredible how your environment can influence you and the way you feel, both physically and mentally. Start living as the new you and watch like magick how quickly you step into the next level.

Day 14 assignment:

What could you do that you've been meaning to do but haven't done? What might the new version of you want things to look like? Can you go window shopping as the next level you?

Today, see if there's anything in your physical environment you can clean up, organize, get rid of, change around, or somehow improve in a way that reflects the desired outcome you decided you were going to have on day one.

For example, if you want to live on the beach, is there a way to adorn your desk with some shells or sentimental pictures of the beach, or can your color scheme in the bathroom reflect an island paradise?

What sort of changes, little or big, can you make in your space that when you look at will remind you of why you're doing this in the first place. Where can you clean up some clutter?

When you "clean things up" you tend to receive clarity and guidance because you are more able to see it now that things have moved out of the way.

What *is* cluttered in your physical life? Can you look deeper and perhaps find a connection with a pattern?

For example, if all your bills are strewn in a pile on the corner of your desk and haven't been touched in three months, perhaps there's an underlying money story you might want to explore. Maybe there's the classic "I'm broke," "I can pay this *or* that," or it could be that no payments were made at all because of overwhelm and not knowing where to start.

What could be an underlying story or conditioned program?

Make a list of all the places where things feel cluttered. What stories are you telling yourself?

Get honest with yourself here and see if you can find any links. This will propel you through much faster than if you're unwilling to acknowledge and address a part of you you've been avoiding. And if you're unwilling to go there, then be with that. There's no right or wrong, nor is it a race to the finish. Just notice what you notice and be kind with yourself during the process.

Daily Affirmation
My environment supports me and is conducive to my success.

Day 15: Play Dress Up

Did you know that the brain doesn't know the difference between what's real and what's imagined? It takes emotional experiences "at face value" and stores the information in the body. That's why when you have a painful experience in life and think about it, you can often feel the emotional charge. The body responds as if you are reliving the experience and activates the pain, even though you are just activating an imaginary event, aka the memory.

Stay with me here.

Working through deep feeling and visualization is a portal to the unmanifested, and a gateway to alignment. When you imagine the outcome already having happened, you alert the body that a shift needs to occur to match this timeline. Your cells receive different instructions as they adjust to vibrate at this new frequency. The moment you accept the feeling is the moment you become a new person.

This is a time to connect on a deep cellular level with your dreams. By connecting like this, you are changing your body's physiology, which literally makes you show up in a different way. Your cells have been given new instructions and because your brain doesn't know the difference between what's real and imagined, it starts looking for proof that your new life is already here.

Quantum shifting is occurring and you are connecting with that new reality, which is already taking place right now. In order to access that timeline, you must fully leave any vibrations, patterns, and beliefs that

Day 15: Play Dress Up

you are still the old version of you. You can't bring any of it with you or you will be contradicting your request.

Your body has to follow your feelings, that's the way it goes. So when you feel deeply into the kind of person you'd be after you achieve your goal, you start changing your reality because you're changing your thoughts, which in turn changes the *feelings*, which are the key to the true magick of manifestation.

And as you change your thoughts, you're changing your beliefs, as beliefs are just thoughts you continue to think. As you upgrade your beliefs, which are self-fulfilling prophecies, your subconscious mind starts filtering your life experience through this new lens.

When you imagine yourself having achieved your goals and living your dream life, put yourself fully into it with your body. Notice what you feel, taste, smell, hear, sense. Allow your body to experience what it *feels* like to be living the experience right now. This sets in the belief that it's possible to manifest this reality. When you feel it *can* be possible, opportunities to make it real start showing up, especially when you stay in this elevated feeling as long as you can.

Day 15 assignment:

Step into your imagination and play like a child today. Wear the energy of the new you like you would try on clothes playing dress-up. Act like the new you, even if for only for one minute. The more you are willing to step into this energy, the faster your manifestation will be.

This is you trusting the universe will provide you with the resources necessary to make things happen.

Dress like the new you would dress. Walk like the new you would walk. Put on makeup, wear a suit, read the newspaper, go to yoga, test drive the camper, search for yurts. Be in the energy of the version of you that's crushed their goals and is living large and in charge.

You don't have to leave the house, but you do have to be willing to be this version of you for a little while, no matter how ridiculous you may feel. Let your imagination run wild and give yourself permission to let nothing be off limits.

If you work from home and are used to being in sweats, get dressed up for the day. If you're looking to move, take a cruise around a new neighborhood or go shopping in a different town. Allow yourself to be that new person for the day and just notice how it feels.

Bonus:

Now, imagine you're getting interviewed by your dream show or magazine. They ask you, How did you do it? How did you go from where you were to this wildly successful person? Can you take us through the steps? What did you do first? What was the hardest step?

What did you have to overcome to get here? What did you learn along the way?

Was there anything you didn't think you would be able to do? How did you handle those challenges?

Day 15: Play Dress Up

What advice do you have for anyone looking to do something like this for themselves?

Answer these questions as the future version of yourself. Make up the answers. Let them be as wild or realistic as you like. Who knows, you may even find an action step in there for yourself you didn't think of.

Step into and try on the energy of the future. How does it feel to show up this way? What do you like best about it? Is there anything that gives you angst about becoming this person?

Give yourself permission to play. Remember, you'll never know if you like something unless you try it. By playing dress up you get to see what works and what might need tweaking when it comes to manifesting your dreams.

Daily Affirmation
I am willing to step into my highest self.

Day 16: Be Uncomfortable

How was it yesterday, stepping into the energy of the new you? Was it exciting? Did anything come up for you that felt uncomfortable or like *there's NO way this could be me*?

If so, great! That means you're growing! Friction walks alongside growth, so when you're experiencing discomfort, that's an opportunity to look within and see what can be energetically cleared to make more space for what's trying to come through.

How uncomfortable are you willing to get for what you want? Are you willing to have those hard conversations and speak your mind? Are you open to things being a complete flip to all that you've previously known?

A lot of the discomfort comes from fear and us saying we "don't know how" something will happen. We fear that we won't be able to do it — whatever *it* is stretches us beyond our current limits and our brains hit overdrive convincing us we should stay right where we are.

It's too hard, too big, too overwhelming, too crazy, too impossible, it'll take too long, there's too much to learn, blah, blah, blah. Our brains go on and on trying to tell us *not* to do the thing we so desire to do. And often we buy into this trash talk!

We identify with what the ego tells us (stay who you are because that's safer than change), and hook into the discomfort of what it would take to actually change or

Day 16: Be Uncomfortable

accomplish the thing. That discomfort can infiltrate our system as fear, paralyzing us from moving forward.

So what do you do when you're in an uncomfortable place within your growth?

Day 16 assignment:

Allow yourself to be fully in the discomfort.

Being willing to sit with what's uncomfortable and walk with fear are the steps that lead you to that next level. When you're willing to be in the discomfort you are alerting the universe that you're serious about making a change, you're ready to heal what needs to be healed, and to bring it on.

So what's uncomfortable about you stepping up and becoming a higher version of yourself?

Is it being visible? Being heard? Failing? Succeeding? Getting up at 5 am? Maybe making a lot of money or being in a position of power? Perhaps you're afraid your friends and family will think you're crazy because you want to start your own turtle-sitting business.

Whatever it is that feels uncomfortable about your growth is a sign of what could use some healing.

Notice what happens in your body when you think about who you have to become to get what you want in life. What about it ruffles your feathers a bit?

Whatever it is, don't get hooked in the story. See if you can stay completely present in the body and notice where the feeling is residing.

Then, just allow it to be. Follow it with your attention if it moves, and just remain present with whatever feelings come through. There's nothing to "do" other than just sit with it. You're not trying to change anything or make it go away, you're just noticing what's happening in your body when you think about what you want to do, be, or have.

Be willing to fully feel the discomfort of whatever comes up. It will eventually burn itself out and often be gone for good. Test it by bringing your original situation or problem to mind and see how it feels this time around. Keep going until you feel nothing (no emotional charge) when you bring up the thought about being the new you.

Sometimes this works right away, sometimes you may need a few rounds. Time is the only variable, but know that when you sit to do this process, you can have profound results, and often the problem is resolved.

Give yourself some grace with this process. It's not always easy to sit with the discomfort. Take your time and be willing to just see what comes up for you. Know that you can do this anywhere, not just in meditation. Someone cuts you off? Go within and feel it. Afraid to post your offer? Go in and feel it. Get in touch with your body and allow yourself to acknowledge what needs to be released.

Daily Affirmation
I sit with my discomfort knowing the way out is in.

Day 17: The Power of Words

I've said it once and I'll say it again (Ok, I say it like *all* the time), words have immense power.

Your words become your thoughts, your thoughts become your beliefs, and those are directly linked to your feelings, which suggest your actions, and all that put together determines your reality.

What you say to yourself, about yourself, and to other people regarding who you are, how you are, and your ability to live out your purpose here give you a huge clue as to what you're *really* asking for.

We've already uncovered some of your excuses and negative self talk. You've turned around some of your personal catchphrases to be more helpful to you. You've put your dreams and desires down on paper and have chosen words that resonate with you, and hopefully you've been repeating them on the daily.

And even if you're not, that's ok because today is ALL about repetition.

Repetition is a key component in manifestation. Think about the water that erodes the river banks — or even the damn Grand Canyon! That's a LOT of repetition, slowly wearing down something seemingly as solid and unmovable as rock.

Look at your belief system like that too. It's been in place for *soooo* long, playing an important role in your life up til now, and it's time for things to change. Change is rarely easy, and we usually meet up with resistance, so by holding tight to your commitment to yourself and anchoring in a willingness to trust, you can ease the pain of transition.

Often it's that in-between time when we're not quite there yet, but we've come too far to go back that causes the most discomfort and questioning of our abilities to succeed.

When we get to a place where our old excuses and programming come in, they are like the powerful river that eroded the banks of your psyche. That pathway is so ingrained that it seems impossible that you could ever change it.

But through repetition and neuroplasticity (the brain's ability to continually learn new things), you absolutely *can* change the course of the "river" (your thoughts and beliefs). A must in this situation is to use words, thoughts, feelings, beliefs, and actions that resonate on the deepest possible level — what I call the "bone buzz."

We talked about this back in the beginning, using words and a phrase that you could feel resonating throughout your body, in order to anchor in the frequency of what you want.

Now, how often are you actually using these mantras, affirmations, turn arounds, etc?

Day 17 assignment:

Today, be a positive parrot. Anytime you tell yourself you can't, you don't know how, you don't feel like it, or someone else rains on your parade, remind yourself why you're doing this in the first place.

Day 17: The Power of Words

Repeat to yourself that your dreams are important and valuable. Use any phrases that feel good and motivate you. Remember that if you don't feel a deep attachment to what you're saying, you most likely have a contradicting belief going on under the surface you might want to explore.

You can always use "soft" words like *willing* or *open* when you don't quite believe something just yet. You can fake it til you make it, but this option helps you get there faster because you are working to anchor something in, not just pretend to feel something you don't.

For example if you're having trouble believing you're a "money magnet" you can say something along the lines of, *I am open to attracting money just like a magnet* or *I am willing to become a magnet for money*. Whatever feels slightly more believable, go with that. Keep revising along the way so that you are always resonating with what you say.

Alternatively, if there's an emotional charge around the word "money" try synonyms like currency, wealth, abundance, riches, and so on. Notice how you feel when you use different words because they each will resonate differently due to your experiences, beliefs, and perspectives.

Remember, it's not what you say, it's the *way you feel when you say it*.

If you don't fully believe what you're telling yourself, then you're wasting your time "trying" to manifest something. You've got to be all in, 100%, to bring your dreams to fruition. You can talk til you're blue in the face, but if you don't believe it, you won't achieve it.

Bonus Dive:

What you tell yourself matters more than you know. Try to be kind, supportive, and encouraging to yourself. Surround yourself with people who do the same. What can you say to yourself today that will keep you inspired, motivated, and on track?

Are there any things you need to stop telling yourself or saying about yourself?

What statements can you put on replay that remind you of how amazing, unique, glorious, beautiful, talented, (and *what else?*) you are?

Now is the time to start changing the way you talk to and about yourself, and speak your new reality into existence. Start talking about your *new* qualities — the things you do and values the *new* you has.

Start showing up and acting like the next level you. Let yourself think, feel, and speak like this new you. Listen to the kinds of words this version of you uses.

Allow yourself to speak of yourself as if you have already become this person. Be willing to "play the part" of being a different version of you for a day, or even just a few hours. Repeat mantras throughout your day to anchor in the feeling of this new reality.

Be the actor in the next chapter of your life. You get to write the script. Make it everything you've ever dreamed of and more.

And keep it on replay.

Daily Affirmation
I love the person I am becoming.

Day 18: Resistance

What actions have you taken so far on your path to greatness? Are there things you feel inspired to do but immediately talk yourself out of doing them? Do you have brilliant ideas but never act? Do you fully believe you can even have the life of your dreams?

Resistance comes in many forms — procrastination, avoidance, negative self-talk, that feeling of *oh hell no!*, doubt, fear, worry, anxiety, constriction, tightness, running for the hills…

However resistance shows up for you, it is asking you to take a look at why you might be pushing away the very thing you so desperately want.

Part of the reason we push away what we want is because deep down we may be afraid to have it. Maybe we fear it will be taken away or won't last, we may be treated differently, we don't feel safe having it, what would other people think if we did x, y, z, who would we be if we went out on a limb and did a crazy thing? We deem it safer *not* to have the thing, most often because we don't want to feel something.

What we resist persists, so what would it take to just go with the flow? What's meant for you will find its way regardless, why not make it a little easier for yourself?

Resistance is a chance to acknowledge there's something hindering your progress, and an invitation to explore it some more. Remember, a lot of what we believe to be "true" about the world isn't our truth, it's someone else's (a parent, teacher, society, generational, etc.), so being able to discern what's yours and what isn't will help you turn around what's stopped you in the past.

Fear is the main reason we talk ourselves out of doing things and really kicking ass at life, so notice what comes up for you when you think about what you need to do to have the life you dream of living. Fear, at its core, is really a fear of *feeling*.

Day 18 assignment:

Notice today where you meet up with resistance. What tasks are you resisting? Why? What feelings might you be avoiding feeling? Why?

Is there something your resistance is trying to tell you? Is there something else you need to learn before you can unlock this door and move forward?

Jot down the ways you are resisting certain things. Look for patterns. Perhaps you resist anything sales or marketing related for your business by inconsistent advertising, not making timely offers, or not following up.

Maybe you resist speaking your needs to people by shutting down during a disagreement, silently holding onto anger, or trying to control a situation.

Could there be resistance to feeling deep love for yourself? Do you beat yourself up and say mean things, deflect nice comments, or constantly look for outside validation?

Be willing to see the reason for the resistance and call yourself out on your shit.

Knowing *why* you resist certain things will bring you the opportunity to heal them. If you're willing to look below the surface, awareness will be revealed to you, and you can count on some uncomfortable emotions coming up.

Get in and go along for the ride. These things come up because your subconscious inherently knows you're ready to let them go. Don't resist what shows up for you. Welcome it in and get curious as to what it is and why it's there. Allow yourself to sit with the feelings and notice what you notice.

Daily Affirmation
Even though I might not know my next step, I keep moving forward with courage and confidence.

Day 19: Find New Friends

It's said that your circle can make or break you. You are who you surround yourself with.

Who are you hanging out with? Are you constantly around complainers, whiners, and people who are unconscious of a different perspective, or are you seeking out the company of those who are kicking ass out in the world, creating solutions, and making changes?

It's true that when you hang out with successful people doing big things, you raise the standards for yourself and strive to do better. They help you step up your game through inspiration, motivation, leading by example, maybe even some masterminding gets thrown in the mix too.

These people have a no BS attitude about getting things done and creating opportunities for themselves. And guess what else? They've probably failed a million and one times.

The wonderful thing about people who really go for it in life is that they take their "failure" in stride. What many consider to be "failure" is really just a lesson, filled with information about how you can do it better next time, perhaps a skill that needs upgrading is revealed, or a new perspective on yourself or the way you're handling things.

Upgrading your circle to reflect the kind of person you desire to become helps you to grow and stretch your limits so you can reach the level of greatness you literally see around you. It's almost as if you can receive some of their knowledge, like some of their sparkly success

Day 19: Find New Friends

magick rubs off on you through osmosis somehow when you spend time with your next level friends.

Your environment matters and the people you spend time with are part of it. Your social environment makes up a part of your physical environment, but also they can influence your thoughts and beliefs, in your mental environment.

Give yourself permission to surround yourself with the kind of people who talk about their dreams, big ideas, changing the world, and who inspire you to live *your* dreams. Be around people who lift you up and encourage you to step forward into your life. Seek out those already doing what you want to do and learn as much as you can from them.

You get to choose who you spend time with. Choose people who make you feel good.

Day 19 assignment:

Make a new friend.

Go where you're celebrated.

Start noticing any "friends" who only seek to tear you down or make you feel bad about wanting your dreams. Really listen to how people speak to (and about) you, and look at how their actions either help or hinder you from moving forward.

Remember what people do has *nothing* to do with you and *everything* to do with them — their old limiting beliefs, conditioning, and programming drive the bus, *not* what they think of you.

Find new friends, because it's out there waiting for you. Go out physically in the world and hang out where the future you would want to hang out. Strike up a conversation in the checkout line, bookstore, or consignment shop. Hit up some online groups or meetups. Probe your friends' friends and see if you might be interested in getting to know someone better.

Keep yourself open to all new experiences that come your way. Keep saying yes to what you feel called to do, and always be on the lookout for someone who "has information for you." Each person you encounter is here to assist your growth, and there's a great book about it called *The Celestine Prophecy* by James Redfield, which points you to noticing these synchronicities in your life.

Upgrade your circle so you can have the support you need to go out there and claim your space in the world. The more you stay open, say yes, and work to build connections, the more people will show up for you. Trust the people you feel drawn to, and start releasing those who are ready to be let go of. Make room for your new besties to sit at your table.

And never, ever sit where disrespect is being served. You're better than that. Walk alone if you have to until you are so strong in your truth that you become a magnet for people who want to be just like you when they grow up.

Daily Affirmation
I surround myself with people who lift and inspire me.

Day 20: Be a Magnet

If you've ever heard of the Law of Attraction, you know that like attracts like. Becoming a magnet for what you desire means that you change your vibration to meet that of what you are calling in. You do this by consciously choosing your words, thoughts, feelings, beliefs, and actions to be aligned with the reality where you have achieved your manifestations.

Did you know your thoughts can make physiological changes in your body? Same thing with words. There's plenty of science on this and it's fascinating to see how vibrations affect the structure of molecules and atoms. Look up Dr. Emoto's water or rice experiments to see the full scope of what I'm talking about here.

And that's all we are folks, vibration. We are energy. Light and information.

We're all just stardust, baby.

Which is great news! Because we *are* energy, we can manipulate it to our benefit. We can put out a request to the universe, and then we can align with the new vibration of what we want, taking guided action to get it.

Knowing that you can play with energy can help to build momentum, strengthening your magnetism.

What if you could call in all that you need? What if you were open to receive all the people, opportunities, resources, and support you need to achieve your wildest dreams? How would you set things up for yourself in your perfect world?

Whatever you are putting out into the universe is what you will receive back, so all this work you've done up to this point has set some new timelines in motion, which have started to bring you new things, even if you haven't noticed yet.

You can build momentum and become a magnet, supercharging your request, by directing your energy to be completely congruent with what you're creating.

You must be in control of yourself and your energy to do this, and pulling from experiences in the past that were difficult can help motivate you to keep moving forward.

Fear, doubt, and worry pull you into a denser vibration, and when you're focused on these feelings, getting hooked into your old stories, you start to attract more things that trigger the timeline.

Clear out the resistance and find those phrases, thoughts, feelings, actions, and new beliefs that keep you on the vibration of who you are becoming. Give yourself space and grace as you step into this new version of you.

Day 20 assignment:

Supercharge your energetic alignment with your desires. You've already gotten crystal clear about what you want. You've tweaked the way you speak and think. You've gotten in touch with your feelings.

Now, put yourself in that dream life. See, sense, feel, know, or imagine all the people who are here to help showing up in your life. Notice all the resources and opportunities opening up as you visualize, meditate, or journal about having achieved your dreams.

Give yourself permission to celebrate how incredible you are. Give yourself a pat on the back for all the things you've done. Go buy yourself something fun.

Fully sit in this energy of accomplishment and badassery. Soak it in. Ramp up how good it feels to go back and see that yes, you *can* do hard, frustrating, seemingly impossible things.

You've done hard shit before, and dammit, you can do it again. Sure, the discomfort may still be there, but you've got the "past you" cheering you on from the stands. Use the energy from these accomplishments to strengthen your tenacity to stay the course.

Take stock of when you're choosing to show up as the new version of you, and when you slip back into your old, limiting belief system. Awareness is the key to freedom, so when you catch yourself out of alignment you can make a new choice in that moment, even if it's just saying to yourself, *Well, that's an old pattern coming up to the surface. Note to self: investigate later.*

Catch the culprit in the act and you've started the healing and realignment process. Take it a step further and clear it completely out of your energy to create the space to more fully align with what you're manifesting.

Notice where you speak against what you want. Be aware of what's rolling around in your head and what comes flying out of your mouth. Look at where you're saying no to doing certain things.

These are all ways we sabotage our efforts without even knowing it because we are on autopilot. Having a smidgen of conscious awareness opens the possibilities of something different happening, should you choose to break the cycle.

We unconsciously call to us whatever we believe, so you must be absolutely willing to believe you can do, be, or have what you want. Know that it is already yours and you will have it.

Daily Affirmation
__I am consciously creating forward motion.__

Day 21: Create a Plan

Now that you're feeling the effects of the energy you've built up around your dreams and desires, what do you know you can do in order to move forward in a consistent way from now on?

Listening to the guidance that comes through is always helpful, as is giving yourself a roadmap to stay on track. Often it's easy to be "busy," but is that work actually getting you closer to your goal? What actions will move the needle? Which actions make the biggest difference? What could you see yourself doing that you would enjoy? Anything you might need to outsource?

Having a plan gives you a clear path to taking actions and helps you prioritize for the day. Acknowledge that you're never going to get it all done, and stop worrying about it.

Your plan is just that — a plan. It's not set in stone and when you hit an obstacle, you can pivot. And you will 100% have to "pivot, turn, walk, walk, walk" away from some things once you get going because they aren't working for you. And that's ok. Part of creating a plan is also planning for when you will hit those inevitable roadblocks.

So how *do* you plan for unforeseen challenges and obstacles?

You sit down and brainstorm all the possible wrenches that will get thrown in the motor.

What might you expect to run into? What feelings might come up? People or situations you may have to deal with? Old patterns that may get triggered? Will you need more resources or a new skillset? Is there any help you may need to ask for?

When you take the time to plan for the challenges you may or may not face, you are much more equipped to handle these situations with grace and ease because you have a plethora of tools at your disposal.

Day 21 assignment:

Create your plan of movement.

Restate your goal that you are working on for these 30 days. Tweak the wording if you have to so that it resonates at the deepest level giving you that "bone buzz" of excitement.

Now, make a list of 50 steps you could take to get you closer to achieving your goal. Yes, 50. If that's too easy, make it 100. The point is to push yourself to get *really* creative and write down anything that comes to mind, even if it seems silly, weird, or downright crazy. Just write and don't judge.

Take a moment and look over your list. What actions jump out at you or give you a feeling of *yeah, I think I'd like to give this a try*? Circle them and pick one to do today. Go with what feels right to you and don't worry about it not being the "right" step. *Something* is always better than nothing.

Next, make a list of 50 possible challenges, obstacles, or roadblocks you may run into. Again, just write without judgment, even if it seems strange, put it down on paper.

Day 21: Create a Plan

What challenges jump out at you as pretty big possibilities that could happen? Jot down a few ways you could approach the situation from a place of curiosity, how you might be able to extract information without holding onto charged energy, and who you look to for support if and when you hit this block.

Here's an example to get you started.

Goal: *Believe I can easily make the money I need to fully live my dream life. Specifically, $10k a month or better in my own business working from anywhere in the world.*

Possible action steps:
1. Take a class on finance
2. Read some books on finance and business
3. Talk to an accountant
4. Heal my fears with the Peace Process* or Instant Miracle*
5. Notice when my disbelief arises- where am I, who am I with, what am I doing
6. Say, *"I can afford that, I am choosing not to buy it now,"* instead of, *"Ugh, I wish I had the money to buy the things I want."*
7. Say, *"I am willing to be open to receiving money from known and unknown sources."*
8. Ask the universe to bring me the money I want
9. Get a job
10. Get another job
11. Pound the pavement and sell my products and services even if I get rejected
12. Look for new places to network

13. Dig up where my old beliefs about money came from
14. Ask the aliens to drop me a bag of cash
15. Look for money to show up on the side of the road
16. Talk to people in my field and see if they have the same fears
17. Talk to people about resources to help a lack-money mindset
18. Find someone who overcame this and work directly with them
19. Pretend I'm super rich for a day and see how that feels
20. Publish content in new places
21. Post my offers every day
22. Pitch my offers personally to people who might be interested
23. Share my offers with potential partners
24. Strike up a collab with someone who has a big audience
25. Get on some interesting podcasts

Possible obstacles:
1. Old thought patterns coming back in telling me I can't
2. Looking at my bank account and seeing a low number
3. No one takes me up on my offers
4. I get rejected
5. The IRS takes all my money
6. I lose my home because I can't make payments
7. The electricity gets shut off because I didn't pay the bill

Day 21: Create a Plan

8. My credit score goes down due to late or missed payments
9. I don't bring in any money this week
10. I'll have a big expense like my car breaking down
11. My laptop dies
12. I'll never be able to change because the pattern is so deep
13. Feeling bad about charging for my services
14. Not wanting to take money for nothing
15. Not asking to get paid for things people ask me to do that I normally would charge for
16. Giving friends things for free
17. Expectations of friends and family getting things for free
18. "You're a healer, this should be free"
19. Stolen identity and hacked accounts
20. Feeling like it will never happen
21. Preaching to the choir
22. Being in the complete wrong market with the wrong message
23. Limited resources
24. Hanging out with/ being around people who think small
25. Buying into the friends and family who want to pop my balloon

Possible solutions:
1. When old patterns come in, I will stop them in their tracks by recognizing it's just a pattern. I will take a breath, acknowledge the pattern, do some healing, and reach for a better thought and feeling.

2. I will notice what comes up for me when I look at my account and see less than desirable numbers. I will heal what I can on the spot, and remind myself my worth is not determined by how much money I currently have. I will remember that this is temporary and I am working to make things change. Then I will allow myself to feel what it would be like to have the amount I want, anchor in that energy, and look for proof money is available to me from known and unknown resources.

3. I remind myself that building a business is a process, and that building relationships is an integral part of being an entrepreneur. I will revisit any possible collaborations and networking that may be available, and reach out to others in the community to get to know them. I promise to myself I won't give up on my dream because it's mine for a reason.

Keep these lists handy. Use your action step list everyday and choose at least one activity to prioritize. You also might want to journal about how each action step worked and if you ran into any challenges along the way. This will help you discern which actions can be the most beneficial to use on a regular basis.

Daily Affirmation
I am committed to doing whatever it takes to make my dreams come true.

Day 22: Relax

Take a deep breath. Sink into your body. Close your eyes for a moment and just breathe.

There is nothing to worry about. Everything is just as it should be.

When we relax and loosen our grip on life, we open ourselves up to the flow of the universe. If we are spending our time in worry, anxiety, and fear, all flow is constricted or closed off, and unable to reach us.

This is the part of the Law of Attraction that might be the most difficult. Letting go of our grip on the outcome. Have faith in the universe that your dreams will be delivered when you let things unfold in the way they are meant to.

Imagine you order something from Amazon. You'd place your order and go about your life knowing your package will be delivered in a day or two. The universe works the same way — ask and you shall receive.

However, silly humans we are, we don't believe that we will receive our order. We fear we've asked for too much, don't deserve to have what we want, worry about what other people will think, we focus on *not* having it, perhaps that it will be taken away, or that it's a ridiculous idea after all.

Then we start to fret that it hasn't arrived yet. The worry sinks in deeper that we won't have our request fulfilled. We start to dig up the seed that *was just planted* to check if the roots have started to grow.

Doing this shows the universe that you're not fully in faith. You can not be open to receive *and* worry you won't get it at the same time.

Quite often the focus is on something *so* specific, all other possibilities of it coming to you shut down.

If you focus too much on the specifics (and yes you *need* to be specific with your request, but not with your outcome), then you're limiting the realm of potential possibilities. You are telling the universe that you think you know better, and that *your* way of receiving is the *only* way.

For example, if you wanted to manifest $5,000 but you only thought it could come from getting a bonus in your next check for working a bunch of overtime hours, then you close the door on it possibly coming to you as a gift, a refund, backpay, finding it in a random spot, creating a new path of income, getting paid for what you love to do, or helping someone with something.

Getting uptight about whether or not you'll get that bonus check, waiting for it to come in, or wearing yourself out working day and night only pulls you out of your state of flow. What if you could just make your request, go about your day doing what you know how to do with an open heart, and allow yourself to look for proof your order is on the way?

Relax and know the universe is working in your favor to bring you what you want. Quite often you will receive validation in the form of signs and feelings, and noticing these things opens you up to receiving even more.

Remember that the universe works in mysterious ways and how something comes to you is usually very

Day 22: Relax

different than what you would expect. This is why it's important to relax and stop worrying about how and when your order will be filled.

What if you could sit back and just *know* your request is on the way the moment you release it to the cosmos? Could you have that much trust and faith that once you've made your decision, committed to having it, cleared the resistance, and started taking some sort of action, things will start to shift in your day to day life? Can you open yourself to believe that signs will show up to prove your order is on the way?

Day 22 assignment:

Notice where you might be anxiously focused on your request. Is there anywhere you might be holding on too tightly to the *need* to have it? When you come from a place of lack (*the rent is due, OMG I don't have the cash, what am I going to do*, *cue freakout*) you carry that energy to your request and the universe responds accordingly.

If you're freaking out because you have a *need* then your delivery will include more need. Focusing on the lack of something keeps you in lack. Your outcome here is need because that's where your energy is — it's on the fact you *don't* have something and you're relying on a wing and a prayer that you'll get it, and you may or may not even believe it will show up.

However, if you let go of that need, and come from a place of faith, you will most likely attract the money and whatever else you're looking for. If you say, *I will do anything and everything I know how to do to get the money and if I still don't have enough I'll ask for an extension. I can figure this out. I've made money before and I can make money again. I know money can come from known and unknown sources and today I'm staying open to all inspiration I receive.*

Can you see how this mindset reframe opens you up whereas a freakout shuts you off?

Where are you getting caught up in the *how* or *when*? Can you build your trust and *know* that when you're aligned, your request is on the way? Are you willing to follow the inspiration you get and take guided action? What can you let go of that might be keeping you worried your request won't be answered? Is there anything else shutting you off from receiving?

Make a list of everything that may be standing in your way of fully relaxing into the trust and faith the universe is asking of you. No matter how big or small it may seem, being aware it's there allows you the opportunity to heal it once and for all. Work on noticing when these fears, doubts, and worries arise, and see if you can catch them in the act.

Go inside and give yourself permission to fully feel into anything that comes up, because when you come from a space of peace, free from worry, you put yourself in receptor mode. By freeing any trapped resistance, you create the space to align with your outcome, and make yourself available for whatever wants to come through.

Relax and receive.

Daily Affirmation
I am at ease knowing my request was received.

Day 23: Detox

Now that you have a list of steps, obstacles, outcomes, and have been walking in the energy of who you want to be, take a look at what you've been noticing showing up for you.

Have you been receiving more opportunities congruent with what you want? Have you met new people who turn out to be *exactly* the people you need? What have you come across that has helped propel you forward unexpectedly? Are there new inspirations you've been following?

When you're in alignment, the universe works with you to manifest your desires. You get in the flow. Time seems to stand still when you're doing the things you love and you're fully present. The warm fuzzies are all around and you're feeling *goooooood*.

Being in full alignment is what will make your dreams a reality. Keeping your faith strong, saying yes to doing the things that feel good and move you forward, opening up to new awareness, seeing a new perspective, and checking yourself before wrecking yourself locks you into the frequency of fruition.

However, one ounce of incongruence sets the ship on a different course. When sailing, one degree change can cause a boat headed for Portugal to end up in Morocco! Don't let that happen when putting in the effort to manifest your dreams.

How do you avoid this misdirection and actually port at your desired location?

Get rid of everything that isn't congruent with what you say you want. That means people too.

Anything going *against* what you want must be removed if you are to call in your request. As of right now, you are no longer available for anything that doesn't move you forward.

You have to make space energetically to receive what you've asked for. If there's something blocking it— a naysayer friend, a belief that you can't, an unwillingness to take action because of fear, whatever — you are giving mixed signals to the universe.

Take a look at your surroundings. Are you in a physical environment that supports where you want to go? How about your mental environment? Are your words, thoughts, and beliefs lined up to work together or are you talking down to yourself and your dreams? Do you have the right people to support you or are you surrounded by Debbie Downers and Negative Nancys?

What do you need to succeed? Make sure you have it and then give a big fat "NO" to everything that doesn't fall into that category. Start surrounding yourself with what's in alignment and keep those boundaries strong when it comes to anything (or anyone) that attempts to pull you down.

Day 23: Detox

Day 23 assignment:

Take a closer look at your life. What supports your dreams that you already have? Make a list of all the things you already have and are doing to move forward.

How does your environment support you? Are you surrounding yourself with the right people who lift you up and inspire you?

Next, see where you are sitting in a pile of trash. Other people's expectations, your old programming, clutter, negative self-talk, bubble bursting friends and family, a lack mindset, fear, overwhelm, and the like, are all incongruent with you being a badass manifestor.

Where are you saying yes to things you really want to say no to? Are you letting other people dictate what you should do? Listening to other people's doubts and fears? Believing that others need to understand your journey or comparing yourself to those farther ahead?

These are all things to detox from your life.

Anything or anyone that does not support your dreams needs to go. Otherwise you'll still be holding onto a thread of your old self. If there's any connection to that small part of you that's afraid to play with the big kids, it will infiltrate the system and wreak havoc.

You *have* to let it all go. Yes, ALL of it. You can't move forward if you've got one foot in the past and refuse to step out of the concrete before it dries because you're scared to be someone new.

Your past doesn't define you. Stop bringing it with you everywhere you go. You're changing, and you made the commitment on Day 2 to do *whatever it takes, no matter what.* Well, this is what it takes if you want to make your dream life come true.

Daily Affirmation
I surround myself with people and things that support my life vision.

Day 24: Remember

You've come a long way from where you were. You've made shifts, seen new perspectives, and have taken action. You're so close you can taste it!

How good does that feel?

Sink into the feeling for a moment and allow yourself to fully be in it.

There still may be a long way for you to go, but seeing how far you've come and anchoring in the fact you're growing can help shoot you forward in a big way.

Inevitably you will run into obstacles and challenges. Things won't go your way. You'll try and it won't work. There'll be frustration and anger. You'll question why you even did this in the first place.

All that's just the universe testing you to make sure you're serious about this new life you say you want. Bumps in the road are to be expected, as nothing in this reality is smooth sailing all the time.

Tests to your tenacity force you to face your fears about your ability to overcome anything that gets in your way.

Plowing through the overgrown field of weeds in your way requires you to hold onto your *why* like a Chinese finger trap. If you don't have that strong connection to the whole reason you're doing this, then you'll likely quit with the others — when shit gets hard.

Most people give up at the point right before their success blossoms. Overwhelm, doubt, and worry creep back in when they don't see the results they want as fast as they want, so they throw their hands up and walk away because they think it's "not happening for them."

Meanwhile, the universe is about to drop the gift to push them over the edge into glory.

Thing is, when we're about to face great change, there's friction around the current situation. Growth *requires* friction to push the new life through. Think about birthing a baby and all the "rubbing up against" the surface that happens when barrelling down the birth canal!

It takes a tenacious person to stay the course when this friction comes knocking at the door. And trust me, it's guaranteed.

The way to overcome this is to remember your *why*.

Day 24 assignment:

Where are you on your journey? Have you experienced this uncomfortable, perhaps even overwhelming feeling of growth? The *OMG, what the hell am I doing, can I even do this anymore because it's so hard and I JUST. WISH. IT. WOULD. HAPPEN. FOR. ME. ALREADY. DAMNIT!*

If that's you right now, then it's time to simmer down and take a breath. We ALL reach this point at one time or another, and it's a golden opportunity to check back in with yourself and reconnect.

Remember why you wanted to do this. Ask yourself if any of your reasons have changed. Grab a

Day 24: Remember

notebook and list all the reasons why this is important for you to do/be/have.

After you write (or as you write), feel into each of these reasons. Remember, the *feeling* is the magick.

For example, if you're working to change your money mindset and your "why" is to be financially free, go even deeper into what that would mean for you. Why is it important to your life that you be financially free? What would that do for you? What would that change? How would you show up? What benefits would you get from having this freedom?

You've felt deeply into your *why* before, now you're adding another layer going into all your reasons. This energy compounds and strengthens your vibration. Remembering why you started down this path keeps you connected to source so you can continue to receive assistance from the universe.

When the going gets rough, and it will, remembering all the reasons you're doing this in the first place will give you the strength to keep going. Your body remembers everything so when you hit a roadblock, you can pull the strength from within to move past it.

Deeply feeling into all the reasons why you've decided to do this anchors the energy in your physical body. Just like when you remember a difficult time in your life and it can bring up all sorts of emotions. It feels like you're literally reliving the situation (because you *are*), and instead by remembering a positive thought brings up a strong, higher frequency for you to tap into is how you spiral up.

Once you've anchored in these positive vibrations and can get that "bone buzz" when you think of all the reasons why you committed to change, you can use this to combat those feelings of doubt, worry, fear, stress, and overwhelm that come up when you're rubbing up against growth.

Anytime you feel the urge to shrink back or play small, **remember** why you made the commitment to yourself. **Remember** all the things that are and will be coming to you when you make room for them. Don't look at what you may be leaving behind, **remember** that your greatest fortune lies on the other side of your fear.

Daily Affirmation
There's a real good reason I'm doing this.

Day 25: Have Gratitude

You've probably heard by now that gratitude is a superpower. Appreciation for what you already have opens the door for you to receive even more to appreciate. What you give out is what you get back, so when you're dishing out gratitude you'll be served back a big old plate of *get-outta-town-this-is-really-for-me*?! (Cue squeals of delight).

Having gratitude for the things you *don't* yet have is the magick to manifestation. If you focus on the fact you don't have something, you are putting out energy to keep it away. Remember, the universe listens intently to your request, doesn't work in negatives, and requires you to create space to receive.

If you're constantly saying, "I don't want to have to go on any more bad dates," or "I don't want to get sick," what are you really asking for? Shitty dates and a case of the sickies.

Focusing on the lack of something in your life alerts the universe that you don't really want it. When you're saying something like "I'm broke, I can't afford that," the universe responds with more situations to keep you in that loop, proving to you that you'll never be able to afford what you want because you're always broke.

Your words are extra important here, as are the thoughts you allow in. But it's your *beliefs* that run the show, so if you believe you're broke, then that's exactly what you'll be.

Turn that around and say, *"I'm so thankful I'm in the process of calling in the money to buy this,"* or *"I am willing to change my money story, even if I don't know how,"* and the energy around the belief that you're broke starts to change.

This act of infusing some graciousness into the fact you don't yet have what you want creates the space for it to come in. Gratitude opens you up to be on a receiving frequency, and as you give without the expectation of receiving, the gifts you do receive bring much to appreciate.

Finding proof that what you want is already here is a powerful way to use gratitude in a supercharged way. When you are willing to believe the universe is already working in your favor, trust that your order is on the way, are grateful for the waiting period (so you can take action and work on clearing blocks), and can get excited for the little things that show you're on the right path, being thankful amplifies the process and your reward is more than you could have ever imagined.

A little gratitude goes a long way. Infusing thankfulness into your tasks is a great way to supercharge your request. You know you have to take action to catalyze the co-creator process, so when you're following your divine guidance, do it with a gracious heart. Especially the tasks that you find difficult, frustrating, and overwhelming.

Most often we get pulled back easily into our old ways. Keep a vigilant watch on your thoughts and feelings when working towards achieving your goals. Complaining about what you have to do, or speaking about how you hate this or that lowers your vibration.

Day 25: Have Gratitude

Feeling icky, angry, and resentful also will bring down your energy.

Where can you take a minute to stop and smell the roses? Slow down and appreciate what you have, where you are, what you're doing, the fact that you *can* do it, all that you've done so far, how you feel, the progress you've made, the synchronicities that are showing up for you, and let's see, what else?

There's so much to be grateful for, and gratitude is a choice. You can choose to be thankful for everything that happens for you in life, or you can choose to let life rule you as if you were a victim to its brutality. However you choose to see it, that will be your reality.

Day 25 assignment:

Make a list of 100 things you're grateful for. Big things, little things, even silly things like the plastic charm necklace from the 80s that hangs in your bedroom even though you're a grown ass adult.

List it all!

Get thankful for all that makes your life enjoyable. Be thankful for the roads so you can drive wherever you'd like to go, the people who made the roads, the lines on the road that (mostly) keep people in check, the car you're in, the amazing technology that made it possible to propel yourself down the highway at 80mph, the gas that powers your car, the people who made that possible, etc...

Get on a gratitude spiral. When you focus on this feeling, you easily attract more of the same, and can find yourself being bombarded by the energy of appreciation. You can literally feel your body change and fill up with love, warmth, wholeness, joy, bliss, compassion, and maybe even some tingles.

For the next five days, make a list of 25 things you are grateful for each day. Try not to have any repeats. Notice what you notice over the course of these last five days and jot down anything that stands out to you. Take stock of what's different after spending some time giving thanks for all that you have and all that is coming to you.

Bonus:

Keep an ongoing gratitude journal throughout the year. Try not to repeat things as you enter at least 10 things a day you are deeply grateful for. Feel into each one as you write and you will continue to be blessed.

Daily Affirmation
Thank you, thank you, thank you, thank you, thank you!

Day 26: Be Present

Louise Hay was known for saying, "the power is in the present." Eckhart Tolle wrote a book about the present moment being all you have, called *The Power of Now*. The present is a gift and it truly is powerful.

Think about how many times a day you are present. Fully present, in your body, clear mind, balanced body. If you're like most people, this isn't a state you're very familiar with.

Rambling thoughts barrel over and over, racing through our minds a mile a minute, and so often we get caught up in this wheel, whisked away to our mind-trap, preventing us from being present. Listening to these stories we tell ourselves day after day causes us to identify with the mind, rather than being led from the feeling-body.

The body is our main instrument and source of collecting information. We see, taste, touch, hear, feel, and sense. Experiencing the world comes from our physicality — you can't experience a rollercoaster in your mind the same way you could if you were strapped in — feeling yourself being toted up that first hill and released, screaming, with your face in the wind as the cart rolls down the tracks at what seems like warp speed. When you simply think about something, it is an entirely different experience than if you were actually there.

Getting out of the mind and into the body takes effort as we have been conditioned for so long to avoid our feelings. It's "too much" for some people to actually feel emotions in their bodies and to be around others who are overly expressive. We avoid, deny, push down, and forget about what needs to be felt (so it can be processed), and it all ends up getting stuck energetically in the body.

Being present means experiencing life through your senses. Forgetting the mind chatter and calling it out for what it is — useless ego tactics. Allowing yourself to fully experience what's in front of you moment to moment is the ultimate goal of being present. And it starts by giving yourself the opportunity to really *feel* from your body.

Presence doesn't mean there are no thoughts in your head, it means the thoughts are either consciously noticed and passed on, or thoughts are intentional — meaning you direct them yourself. The mind is at peace and you are not getting hooked back into your old stories.

Why do we avoid being present? Because we don't know how to sit still. We've been taught throughout our lives to keep looking to the future, we've been taught to not feel, that it's too uncomfortable to sit with our emotions, and this hustle culture we live in tells us to devote all our attention to work, achievements, and how *that* is what brings happiness and success. We've been told to "work hard," to save up for retirement so that "someday" we can actually enjoy our lives.

WHAT?! *Wait to enjoy your life?* That's the most absurd thing I've ever heard. No one is promised tomorrow, so wouldn't it make more sense to start enjoying your life *now*? What are you waiting for?

The ego (as is reflected in human life patterns) lives in the past and bypasses the present to create a "safe" future based on the previous life experiences we've had. This creates expectations of what's to come in the future. Being present in the moment takes us out of cycle and into a place of true awareness, which is also our personal power of creation.

Day 26 assignment:

Breathe. Feel the air entering your body, filling up your lungs. Notice your chest and stomach rise and fall as you inhale and exhale. Listen to the breath as it enters and exits your body. Feel the coolness of the air when you breathe in and the warmth in the release. Allow yourself to follow the air from your nose to your toes as you deeply inhale, and flow back up your body as you gently exhale.

This breathing exercise is one of the easiest ways to get present. What did you notice when you were doing it? How did your body feel? What was happening in your mind? Is there a difference in the way you felt before and the way you feel now?

Go back and reread, following along, and see how deeply you can follow your breath into your body. Doing this connects you physically and anchors you into your body. Notice what you notice without trying to control anything.

Stopping to take a breath brings us back into the present moment. It gets us out of our heads, out of reaction mode, out of identification with an intense emotional trigger, and gives us room to craft a response.

Creating space for yourself is part of the act of being present. It means you aren't using a conditioned, autopilot reaction to what you're experiencing. You take in the experience consciously when you are present, seeing it for what it is, and from a place of balance you respond in a way that is accepting and beneficial. Having this space gives you a much easier chance of being understood and communicating your point of view in a clear, non-aggressive way.

Walking through your day totally present brings you a different perspective on life. Time slows down. You feel different. Your surroundings become brighter, crisper, more vibrant. You see things you never realized were there. New thoughts enter your awareness, and you start noticing your body more. There's a sense of peace that follows you.

Where are you not being present in your day to day life?

Are you overwhelmed with your to-do list or an argument you had with someone? Are you still upset from the person who cut you off on the highway or that you have an extra bill to pay? Are you lost in your frustration of something you can't seem to figure out, or worried about how you're going to tell a friend some bad news? Are you caught in a story about yourself that's been on replay for years, maybe even decades? Still have anger towards the kid on the playground that bullied you in elementary school?

These are things that zap your presence. Notice today where you are getting caught up in your stories from the past or worries about the future. Notice where you're still reeling from things that happened, and where

Day 26: Be Present

you're creating anxiety about what you imagine could happen. Awareness is the key to freedom, so when you catch yourself getting carried away, come back to the breath, create some space, and notice how you feel.

Remember, the present moment is all you have.

Daily Affirmation
The present moment is beautiful, safe, and powerful.

Day 27: Reflect

We're in the home stretch! Just a few days left of fully anchoring in these new habits of awesomeness that you have been creating for yourself.

How far have you come since you started this journey?

So often we don't give ourselves credit for all the work we've done, the obstacles we've overcome, and for committing to ourselves to be better. We minimize our efforts like they're no big deal, but guess what? They *are* a big deal.

Celebrating your wins is extremely important as it redirects you back to you. You have to be your biggest cheerleader when it comes to making these personal changes, so be sure to give yourself a pat on the back for doing the work to get to where you are.

Reflecting on your progress gives you an opportunity to pick out the things that propelled you forward. It gives you insight as to what unconscious patterns were at play, and if they are still trying their best to sabotage your efforts.

Sitting down to do inner work reveals information to us in layers. We get to go deeper into the process of uncovering our patterns, programs, and conditioning in order to know ourselves better. Reflecting on who we were versus who we are today holds so much value when it comes to stepping into the highest version of yourself.

Granted, who you were yesterday no longer matters because the past is gone. It no longer exists. And with that dissolution of existence in time, the version of

Day 27: Reflect

who you used to be dissolves right along with it. Every experience we have shapes who we are in a way, and we have the choice as to how we let it affect us. We can hold on to and identify with the pain, or we can extract the wisdom and repurpose the energy.

Staring at your reflection allows you to see the changes you've been making. Even if you don't feel like things are happening, they are. Quite often we don't realize what's getting stirred up energetically in order to make space for what we desire to come in. You might actually glow.

Looking back over the past few weeks and reflecting on steps you've taken, awareness you've gained, patterns you've healed, or guidance you've received helps you track your success. There's no possible way you didn't move forward, so where can you point out some moments of change?

It's time to take a good look in the mirror and get honest with yourself about where you're at, where you've been, and where you're going.

Day 27 assignment:

Grab your journal because it's time to write. Give yourself some time with this one because *you* are important. You are valuable and your progress matters. Everything about you matters so stop judging yourself and your actions. Allow yourself to open up and be vulnerable and honest about who you are in this moment.

Remember, the present is all you have. You have the ability to choose change, (awareness is the first step in being able to recognize it), and you can act on that new choice at any moment.

Where can you notice multiple choices showing up for you? Are you able to choose something different when you circle back to the situations that keep showing up in your life? Have you made a choice to step out of your comfort zone, even just to dip your toe in a new puddle?

Take some time to notice who you have been. Write a list of all the things that made you this person and how they caused you to feel and show up in the world. These attributes might be the reason you chose to tackle this program — because you recognized something about yourself that was keeping you stuck, and *knew* it was time for change.

Now, take a look at who you are. Go stand and look in the mirror and see yourself as a different person than you were yesterday. What's been inspiring or motivating you to show up in a new way these days? How are you making more aligned choices about your future? Have you noticed any physical changes occurring in your body lately?

Reflect back over the past few weeks and see where you have changed. How are you different now? Do you recognize the person you used to be? Can you embrace this old version of yourself with love and compassion? What do you love about who you used to be and how you've changed? Are there things you still don't want to or can't seem to let go of?

Get it all out then answer this question:

Day 27: Reflect

What has this journey taught you so far?

You've come a long way from where you started, whether you know it or not. Sometimes the energy needs to be pushed around to make room for you to reach your next level, and once the space is cleared, watch out because the floodgates open!

Daily Affirmation
Just for today, I am willing to recognize my greatness.

Day 28: Keep the Faith

Part of manifesting requires you to trust that once you ask, you will receive. It is essential to work from faith, believing that what you've requested is on the way, keeping an open heart and mind as the universe works in your favor.

Regardless if you've seen massive, life changing shifts or not, know that the universe is hard at work to align things just right. We never know when timelines will play out, but when we keep doing our work with blind faith that it's not in vain, the rewards are that much sweeter when they arrive.

Having absolute faith in the universe is what will open up the fortune on the other side of your fear. Taking action and following the inspiration you receive, no matter how unconventional or downright crazy it might seem, alerts the universe that you're willing to keep going because you are *that* determined to make your dreams come true.

When you keep showing up day after day, with zero proof that what you're doing will even work, but have that fire burning within you, anything you do puts out powerful attractors into the field. You vibrate on a high frequency which resonates with what you want, and there can't be any worry or doubt about receiving. There's an inner *knowing* that it will come to you, yet you are not concerned about when or how.

This is what is meant by surrender. Letting go of trying to control when, where, and how something will happen for you. Holding the essence of your desires

Day 28: Keep the Faith

close, doing what you know how to do, and having faith that signs will show up for you.

Flying on a wing and a prayer, *hoping* things will work is different than surrendering. Hoping is rooted in lack, as there is an underlying belief that it might not come, and you're waiting on something else to happen first. With surrender, you have a deep inner *knowing* that something will manifest through you. You don't know what, or how, and that doesn't even matter. You just *feel* that what you do pushes you towards new doors being opened, and you follow, trusting wherever those doors lead.

Day 28 assignment:

Is there anywhere you've lost faith?

Have you been showing up, doing the work, and "not seeing results"? Are you feeling anything less than giddy and blissful when you think about your *why* and what this new thing will bring you?

Take a moment and check in with yourself and see if there's any incongruence still floating around. Remember, any contradictions you're making within your words, thoughts, feelings, actions, and beliefs will throw off your frequency, giving you wishy-washy results.

If you're feeling like you've lost some faith or could use a boost, think back to a time when you really, *really* wanted something, and you got it. Maybe you asked, maybe you worked extra hard, maybe you conjured up unique and out of the box ways you could make things happen for yourself. Maybe you just dropped big hints. Whatever you did, it worked. You've done it before, and you can do it again.

Have you seen any proof saying you're on the right path? What has shifted in the past few weeks for you? Can you notice what's different in your life or the way you act and feel lately? Can you find distinct points where you made a different choice or followed your inspiration and it led you to an opportunity, awareness, or resource of some kind?

Where might you be holding on too tightly to your outcome and not having faith the universe will provide for you? Being afraid to welcome in what's yours will keep you getting small results. Have faith that you will receive and know what to do with your abundance.

Often we push away what we want because we think we won't be able to handle it. Don't believe the lies your ego tells you about your ability to manifest. Keep the belief strong that you can and will succeed in your endeavors. Look for proof everyday that your new life is here for you now.

What you believe will be true for you, so keeping your faith front and center will align you with all that you need to carry out your tasks. Love notes will be dropped into your awareness, showing you whatever you need to know. When they show up for you, give thanks and remind yourself that when these synchronicities happen, it's the universe telling you *I see you working hard for what you want, here's a gift to help you along your way*.

Make a list of all the synchronicities that have shown up for you so far along this journey the past 28

Day 28: Keep the Faith

days. Keep a notebook handy and be sure to jot down when and where you run into these occurrences. It's also helpful to note how you feel and what you were doing when this magick hits.

Remind yourself again why you're doing this. Connect deeply with this feeling, and sit in the energy of it for a while. Ramp it up so you're supercharged, removing any doubt, fear, or worry from your field. Remember that sometimes space needs to be cleared for what wants to come in, so if you haven't "seen results" it's because you have been working on a deep energetic level to release patterns and programs that prevent you from turning your dreams into your reality.

Trust the process and keep your faith stronger than your fear, then watch your dreams blossom.

Daily Affirmation
My dreams belong to me because I am the one meant to make them happen.

Day 29: Hold Tight

"How you do one thing is how you do everything."

This adage basically says that whatever habits you carry with you will be present in everything you do. That is why it's so important to raise your self awareness to recognize these patterns within yourself, give them the attention they want, and heal them for good.

During this program you took a close look at one of your patterns you were aware of that needed to change. Perhaps some others have surfaced for you during this journey, as they tend to do with any form of healing and inner work.

After reflecting on your progress, are you able to recognize how your patterns were preventing you from moving forward? Can you see how your old belief system showed up in every aspect of your life, causing you pain and angst, refusing to give you the results you requested?

These patterns will continue to play out, recycling situations until you learn the lesson. Awareness of the pattern is the first step to releasing it, and being able to catch it at the onset is what will set you free by giving you the opportunity to make a different choice.

What's been ruling your life subconsciously is buried deep within you, and often these sneaky saboteurs keep themselves out of sight, ready to wreak havoc any chance they get. These are the knee-jerk reactions you have when you get triggered. The autopilot responses you give without a second thought. The same old same old ways you deal with things.

Day 29: Hold Tight

How do you handle situations that push your buttons? It's guaranteed that you will be faced with tough decisions, experiences you'd rather not have, and conversations that reveal things you might not have wanted to know, but now you do. Inevitably there will be people who down talk your ideas, thwart your success, and try to keep you as the person *they* want you to be.

There's no avoiding these party poopers, but there's a new you just waiting to show up, ready to change the trajectory of your experience by making a different choice.

Hold on tightly to these higher frequencies you've been anchoring in. When it comes to having to step up and be the change you want to see, each time you act accordingly it becomes easier and easier to show up as the new you.

Day 29 assignment:

Spend the day noticing how you respond to things that happen in your day. Pay close attention to the way you talk to people and handle the encounter. What choices are different with what you say and *don't* say? How do you feel afterwards? Were you able to extract any wisdom, awareness, or information from the situation?

Ask yourself what's different in the way you interact with the world around you. The old you had a way of doing things that created your current life situation, and the new you is creating your future every time you make a different choice.

Where can you clearly see shifts? Pinpoint how the old you would have handled a situation and notice what happens when you act from the more aware version of yourself. What new choices are being consistently made? Has doing this allowed more love notes from the universe to be dropped in your lap? What have those gifts been?

Look back over this last month and see how you've changed. There may be pockets where you've recognized you're different, and there may be a linear record of your growth. Maybe you haven't noticed any changes at all, and that's ok too. Trust wherever you're at, and keep a sharp eye out for anything that reminds you of who you're working to become.

Write down all the ways you can see how you've changed. Maybe you stopped doing something that was unhealthy, took some new risks, changed the way you speak to yourself and others, or had a conversation that was out of your comfort zone.

Becoming someone brand new requires courage and faith. You must trust in the unknown, and transforming into someone you don't know can be extremely scary. But you're doing it because it's *that* important to you. You know your reasons, you're doing all the work, and living everyday with the essence of your dreams in your heart.

Hold on to this new version of you. Old patterns and programs die hard, and will likely try to sneak up on you when you least expect it. Don't let yourself fall back into the trap of who you were (and watch out for people who don't want you to change).

Day 29: Hold Tight

Walk as this upgraded person, this new you, and be willing to step fully into the life you want. Keep your vision strong and your faith unshakable. Hold on to your dreams and desires with the mentality of *I'll do whatever it takes, no matter what, to make this happen.* Let go of the outcome and trying to control things. Let it all unfold as it is meant to.

What other ways can you anchor in the new you?

Daily Affirmation
Every day I am becoming more and more of me, and I love who I'm becoming.

Day 30: Be Tenacious

Today you get to step out into the world as the brightest version of you that you've ever been. And you get to do the same tomorrow, and the day after that, and the day after that.

Be bold enough to hold your head high and remain connected to your "why," saying no to anything that doesn't foster your growth.

An important thing to remember as you move forward is that not everyone is going to understand your journey. Some people may not want you to change because it threatens their existence, their "norm," and they aren't willing to experience change themselves. They might not be ready, they might be fending off fear, or their journey may be one of unconsciousness — the point is you have to hold on to what *you* want, as people will inevitably attempt to pull you back down.

Having the tenacity to be exactly who you want to be will piss a lot of people off, for various reasons. Quite often, because we are mirrors to each other and our environment, when someone changes, it threatens people because they see in you what they themselves (secretly) want to be — a shining star, following their dreams and loving life. For whatever reasons, they have been avoiding this part of themselves and it's triggering to see you as what they so desperately want to be.

Some people lash out when you become someone new simply because they don't understand the journey of personal development and soul callings. And that's ok.

Day 30: Be Tenacious

Again, your mission here is your own, and you don't have to explain it to people who can't grasp the concept.

Ask yourself if it's worth it to keep squeezing yourself into a space where you no longer fit. That too-tight box of other people's expectations and limiting beliefs is no longer your residence. The places where you are misunderstood or feel invalidated or unheard are no longer visited. You're no longer available for relationships you've outgrown.

Be tenacious enough with your upgraded self to remove your presence from where you are not being uplifted. Yes, you will encounter less than desirable situations from time to time as this is part of life, but constantly feeling like crap no longer has to be your default mode.

Tenacious people are successful people because they don't give up. You signed a contract with yourself on Day 2 saying you'd do *whatever it takes, no matter what* to become a better version of yourself. Now it's time to make good on that promise.

Day 30 assignment:

First of all, congratulations for showing up for yourself for 30 straight days. If this is something you're not used to, this accomplishment is worth its weight in gold. Plus, you've made a habit of it, since habits are created in about 28 days. You deserve a big *Hell Yeah* and a high five!

As you walk through your day, be willing to see past what you normally see. Look for the Truth in all encounters. Notice how you feel when you're having different experiences. Those leading you to your next step will feel differently than those attempting to keep you in old patterns.

Use divine discernment and let Spirit guide you through your day. Say *yes* to what feels good, moves you forward, or calls to your soul. Give a big fat *NO* to anything that doesn't resonate. This is *your* growth, so weed the garden bed if you want to fully bloom.

People will absolutely try to hold you back. Notice who does this to you. Perhaps a conversation would help open their understanding, maybe you need boundaries, or a complete change in the relationship. Not everyone will understand, and you need to surround yourself with those who support your growth and vision. You don't have to completely eliminate party poopers from your life, but just be aware of what happens to you after being with them.

Be willing to be unpopular. Use that tenacity to hold on to your dreams when others gift you their crappy opinions. Stand alone if you have to, because you know what's right for you. Trust that when you hold tight to your "why," stay the course through all the storms, and have the brashness to really go for it, the universe will catch you with every leap you take.

Make a list of all the things you love about who you have become. Go back to Day 4 and look over your notes from the first time you dug deep. How does the new you respond to your old excuses? Are these points you wrote

Day 30: Be Tenacious

down still valid or has your perspective changed? What's the best part about where you're at today?

What's the biggest lesson you've learned about yourself? How will this information be useful to you moving forward? Can you glean any other insights about who you are today?

Write about how you will continue to show up as a bigger and better version of yourself everyday. Pick a date in the future and write "a day in the life." Make it as juicy as you can, giving it lots of detail. Feel into the emotions as you write. Dream big because you're the kind of person who can make it happen.

Never forget what a powerhouse you are. Sometimes you may not feel like it, but you're one incredible human. Life ebbs and flows as we row our boats along the stream, so look for where you can lift the paddle and float along the path that ultimately leads you to your destination. It will feel easy, effortless, and will fill you with joy.

Use these past 30 days to boost you when you're in a low spot. Pick a day and trust the message is what you need. Give thanks and appreciation for all that has come and all that will follow. Go do something nice for yourself today, and own the fact you can do nice things for yourself *all the time*.

Nobody gets to live your life for you. *You* are the one who makes the choices and you are in control of what you allow in. Be the vigilant gatekeeper of your inner peace. You've worked so hard to get to where you are today, so keep moving forward. One step at a time.

Daily Affirmation
I am more powerful than I realize.

About the Author

Katie Cavenagh is a writer, tap dancer, and energy healer. She is the founder of The CT Tap Collaborative, teaching improvisation and the history of tap dance. With the pandemic shutdown, and the passing of a company co-founder in early 2020, Katie turned back to her love of spiritual development to begin a new career in energy and sound healing while continuing to follow her dream of being a writer. Always a rebel and on a mission for change, her goal is to help heal the world by raising conscious awareness and empowering people to tap into their own personal magick to create miracles in their lives.

Website: FeelYourLight.com
Read More: medium.com/@katiecavenagh
Email: Katie@FeelYourLight.com

More

Pure F*cking Magick 1:1 Session

Whatever was a problem isn't anymore.

PFM, IRL.
Biz Version

Start your business, grow your business, or take it to new heights with Pure F*cking Magick. Bust through any money blocks, fears of success, or doubts about playing big in the world. Bi-weekly online group calls get you masterminding, healing, coaching, and networking. Starting January 2023

Info for the above can be found at FeelYourLight.com

www.ingramcontent.com/pod-product-compliance
Lightning Source LLC
Chambersburg PA
CBHW070456090426
42735CB00012B/2574